Happy Tabby

Develop a Great Relationship with Your Adopted Cat or Kitten

Susan C. Daffron
Logical Expressions, Inc.

ISBN-13: 978-0-9749245-3-3

ISBN-10: 0-9749245-3-9

Library of Congress Control Number: 2007906436

Warning and disclaimer: This book is designed to provide information about adopting and caring for cats. Every effort has been made to make it as complete and accurate as possible, but no warranty or fitness is implied.

The information in this book is provided on an "as is" basis. Logical Expressions, Inc. and the author take no responsibility for any errors or omissions. The author and Logical Expressions, Inc. also shall have no responsibility to any person or entity with respect to loss or damages arising from information contained in this book or from any programs or documents that may accompany it.

Contents

Adopting a Cat

Cats are the most popular pet in the United States, yet many people seem mystified by the feline creatures with whom they share living space. This book helps prepare you for adopting a cat, explains your choices, so you can select the right cat for your family, and gives you advice on how to deal with challenges you may face when you share your life with an adopted cat.

This book is also based on reality. My cat, your cat, and pretty much everyone's cat is not going to be the perfect model citizen all the time. Like people, no cat is perfect. Most people adopt cats because they are hoping to enjoy companionship and years of cuddly moments with their new feline friend. And for me, sharing my life with my furry critters is extremely satisfying. However, cats are cats; they are not tiny people in furry suits. Expecting them to act in any "human way" is unfair and a primary reason so many cats end up in animal shelters.

For example, your cat does not run away or scratch the furniture out of spite or to be "mean." A cat will do many things because of instinct and nature. My goal with this book is to help explain some of these behaviors and what you can do to avoid or solve problems when they come up.

A recent survey from the American Pet Products Manufacturer's Association says that 90 million people own cats, yet the Humane Society of the United States estimates that only 2%–5% of cats that enter shelters are reclaimed by their owners. In fact, of the estimated 6–8 million dogs and cats that enter U.S. shelters, 3–4 million are euthanized because there are not enough homes for them.

When I was volunteering at an animal shelter and started writing pet columns in our local newspaper, the shelter manager I worked with always said, "don't forget about the cats!" Although cats are generally easier to care for than dogs, they do have a number of basic needs. Like the old joke says, dogs have owners and cats have "staff." Yet people aren't born knowing everything about how to care for cats, so I cover what you need to know in the pages of this book.

Mostly, this book is about understanding and compassion. When you adopt a cat, you make a commitment to caring for her. Your cat may not be perfect, but she is your cat. And I feel sure, you aren't perfect either. You have human foibles, stresses and issues going on in your life. But your cat is depending on you for her day-to-day existence.

If you treat your cat well, you will be rewarded with happy purring, countless cuddly moments, and endless feline entertainment for years to come.

About Me

This book is designed especially for owners of cats that have been adopted from humane societies, animal shelters, or breed rescues. It's about cats that have been given a second chance at a new home, so I don't talk about the latest in "cat fancy" or very much about the various breeds of cats. Realistically, most cats at shelters are "mutts" for lack of a better term.

This book is for people who want to develop a good relationship with their family cat. As a former animal shelter volunteer, veterinary technician, and owner of six shelter critters, I've seen a lot. This book contains my best advice for people like you, who have chosen to adopt, but need specialized guidance on dealing with "previously owned" cats.

This book also includes my personal experiences in solving the problems of my own adopted cats. Like any pet owner, my life with cats has not been completely without incident. I talk about these issues in sidebars that appear throughout the book. The sidebars also contain a few personal reflections on life with my two slightly offbeat tabby companions, Alia and Troi.

With my cats, I have lived through and found solutions for many common kitty problems: such as clawing, yowling, eating bad things, illness, breaking glass, and innumerable other incidents that I've undoubtedly blocked from my memory.

My cats are hardly perfect and I'm not an extraordinary pet owner. In fact, I'm just like you. I like cats and I want to have them in my life. One thing I do realize, however, is that every pet is an individual and you have to work within the limitations of the animal's personality.

For example, years ago, I had a cat named Chani. She was not exactly the sharpest knife in the drawer and she was extremely shy. I didn't expect her to suddenly become a rocket scientist or come out and be gregarious with strangers. It just wasn't in her nature. During her life, she did, however, spend many, many happy hours curled up in my lap. Basically, she was *my* cat and she liked it that way.

If you've ever read a cat book that sounded like it was written by a veterinary committee, you can be sure this one is different. I've lived with and experienced myriad problems with my cats. But now we peacefully cohabitate and life is good. If I can do it, so can you!

Every Rescue Has a Story

As I mentioned, this book is about reality and I refer to my (very real) cats throughout the book. When I worked at an animal shelter, I learned that every rescue has a story. Here is your introduction to the all-feline team:

Alia (gray and white tabby): We adopted Alia and her sister Chani from a group in San Diego called Friends of the County Animal Shelters (FOCAS). This group pulled cats that were on "death row" from the shelters and put them into foster care, so they'd have a better chance at adoption. However, Alia and Chani never spent any time in a shelter because they were fortunate enough to have a mother cat who was found by a FOCAS volunteer in the dumpster in her condo parking lot.

The volunteer took in the momma cat and let her have kittens in a spare bedroom. Then she adopted out two of the kittens to us. We signed all the contracts as if we were adopting the cats from a shelter. Although they didn't enjoy it, the feline team left the sun of Southern California and survived the move to Idaho. Alia is still going strong, but Chani, who was the runt of the litter, died in 2000 from kidney failure.

Troi (brown tabby): We adopted Troi from a humane society south of here because Alia was incredibly depressed after the death of her sister tabby Chani. I never would have believed it if I hadn't seen it, but it seems that cats do grieve. Alia would no longer get up and wander around. All she did was eat, sleep, and cry mournfully. She got hugely fat and we were afraid Alia would just sort of curl up and die. I consulted a behaviorist who suggested getting a kitten who looked as much like Chani as possible. Oddly enough, the shelter only had one tabby in residence at the time: Troi. We took her out of the kennel and played with her for a while. She seemed nice enough, but we decided against adopting her, mostly because we were still so upset about Chani's death.

I put Troi back in the kennel and said goodbye. As I was walking out of the room, I looked back at her. She gave me a look of such disappointment that I turned around. I knew then I had to take her. So we adopted her after all. Named after Counselor Troi in Star Trek, she has done a tremendous job of counseling Alia. And the ironic thing is, even though she was lanky and leggy at 5 months when we got her, she grew up to look almost exactly like Chani, who was a small, rotund cat. It's weird. Even though Troi has a completely different personality, sometimes I think Chani's spirit is in there somewhere. Plus, just like Chani, Troi has discovered that my lap is a fine place to be.

Why Adopt a Cat

As I mentioned earlier, cats are popular. Yet even though so many homes have one or more cats, there still are many more cats than there are permanent, loving homes for them. Because of cats' impressive reproductive capabilities, every year shelters are inundated with homeless cats during "kitten season." Unfortunately, every community has stray and feral cats that aren't spayed and neutered. Cats do what cats do and the result is the yearly onslaught of kittens.

The bottom line is that the best reason to adopt a cat or kitten is to save a life. Staggering numbers of cats are euthanized every year. Most of them are not "bad" in any way. They aren't mean, dangerous, crippled, or sick. In fact, they are probably kittens whose only crime is that they are unwanted and unlucky. If you've decided to make a cat a part of your life, choosing to adopt means you're going to give a cat another chance at a good life.

If you need another excellent reason to adopt, consider this: you'll be lessening the amount of animal suffering in the world. People who give up their cats for adoption often say they "don't have time," the kids "don't help," or they suddenly developed "allergies." What all these excuses really mean is they never anticipated the responsibility of pet ownership. Because of their lack of foresight, the cat is taken to a shelter and his whole world is turned upside-down. When you adopt, you restore happiness and love to that critter's life, which is definitely something to feel good about!

When you adopt a cat, you also do a good deed for your community. There are financial as well as emotional costs associated with tracking down cases of animal cruelty, impounding unwanted or abused animals, and maintaining an animal shelter. When you adopt a shelter cat, you help to ease these community financial and emotional burdens.

The biggest challenge facing animal shelters is pet overpopulation. It's not just during "kitten season" either. Shelter employees hear just about every excuse in the book for people dropping off their pet's "accidental" litters at the back door. The reason this problem continues is obvious: unlike people, cats and dogs don't have just one offspring at a time. One cat or dog that has babies and whose babies have babies can be responsible for the birth of 50 to 200 kittens or puppies in just one year. The reproductive rate of dogs is 15 times that of humans, and the reproductive rate of cats is 30 times that of humans.

Spaying or neutering is the solution to this pet overpopulation problem. It's better for you, better for the community, and (contrary to the endless old wives' tales) much better for the animal as well. It's simple: spayed or neutered animals are better behaved and healthier. Females spayed before their first heat cycle are healthier than those that aren't. (Ask your vet, it's true!)

Neutered male animals are better behaved and have fewer problems with aggression. Neutering reduces roaming and fighting and most animals lose the desire to constantly mark their territory. Animals that have been spayed or neutered also tend to live an average of two to three years longer than unsterilized pets.

Your Cat and You

Many of us live a stressful existence. As you run from place to place with a cell phone glued to your ear, it can be a challenge to just stop for a minute and look at the world around you.

Fortunately, those of us with pets have a live-in example of how to be "in the moment."

Cats don't worry about deadlines and they don't nag you (except maybe for dinner). You may have noticed that a feline sleeping in the sunlight is rarely stressed out. Your cat can be endlessly amused simply by watching an errant insect crawl across the floor or by jumping on a paper bag.

Many studies have shown that owning a pet is good for you. Although a pet isn't a substitute for human companionship, people who have pets are less likely to become depressed. Having a pet forces you to think about something outside of yourself and your own little thoughts. Coming home to feed or play with the cat gives you a sense of purpose and responsibility. Someone is depending on you.

Studies have shown that owning a pet can actually have a beneficial effect on your blood pressure. Apparently those who had adopted a cat or dog had lower blood pressure readings in stressful situations than their pet-free counterparts. Many studies indicate that owning a pet can keep us healthier and happier for longer.

When you have pets, you are never alone. Probably the loneliest time of my life was when I was first married before we got our kitties. When my husband traveled, the house was completely silent. It was the first time in my life I'd ever not had some type of animal in the house, and it was just plain strange. Although cats are often very quiet, it's comforting just to know they are there. And if laughter is the best medicine, pets can be a great prescription for the blues. It's hard to maintain a straight face when you watch a cat do something really dopey like "miss" while jumping up onto the sofa. (It's even funnier to witness the cat indignantly stalk off and pretend she did it on purpose.)

Unfortunately, when this human–animal bond is broken, the results often affect far more than the pets in the family. In homes where spousal or child abuse exists, animal abuse often happens first. In fact, many women who would otherwise seek shelter end up staying with an abuser because of threats to kill the family pet.

Fortunately, the link between animal abuse and family violence is becoming more well known and publicized, so that in some communities law enforcement and animal services are working more closely. Most humans struggle and stress over problems of their own creation. Pets can be a valuable window into a simpler, more peaceful existence. Adopting a pet is a way to add more love into your life and that's certainly a good thing.

Is Adoption Right for You?

The purpose of this section is simple: to make sure you're really ready to take on that shelter cat or kitten.

Acquiring a pet has a big impact on your daily life. Literally millions of cats end up at animal shelters (or worse—on the street) because their former owners didn't stop to think about the impact a cat would have on their daily lives. So even though you may be excited, remember that once you bring home your new cat, your life will change.

Some of the changes will be emotional. You get to enjoy the companionship of the cat, but many shelter kitties may require extra love and patience, particularly at first as she adjusts to your home. Your lifestyle will change as well. Cat hair will end up on the furniture and a small furry life now will be depending on you for her very existence. If you are a jet setter, you no longer can just take off for a couple of weeks without considering the needs of your cat.

The bottom line is that when you get a cat, you will have to make adjustments to your routine, your housekeeping, and your schedule. It's also important to consider the financial realities of pet ownership. Your cat will require food, medical care, and other necessities throughout her life.

If you have children or other pets, you should consider the impact your newly adopted cat will have on their lives. Before you actually start visiting animal shelters, spend some extra time with this section. Try to imagine how life will be different with a cat. This little adoption "reality check" will pay off in the long run for both you and your new kitty.

Should You Get a Cat?

Every spring, adorable kittens seem to appear everywhere. But before you let yourself fall in love, you need to ask yourself a few questions. When you get a cat or kitten you are changing your life for the next 10 to 15 years. Change can be stressful, so think about the ramifications of adding that furry face to your household before you get a pet.

1. Money. Getting a cat costs money. Your new pet needs food and other paraphernalia such as litter, leashes, collars, and toys. Taking your pet to the veterinarian costs more money. It's unfair to the animal to deny him or her these basic needs. If you can't afford the cost of routine upkeep and veterinary care, don't get a pet.

2. Lifestyle. Honestly evaluate the environment you'd be bringing a cat into. Here are a few questions you should ask before you get any pet.

Are you about to make any major life changes, such as having children, moving, marrying, or divorcing?

- Do you travel?

- Does your landlord permit pets?

- Are you away from home all day? If so, do you have time to give a cat the attention it needs?

- Are you healthy?

- Are you allergic to pet hair?

- Do you demand a meticulously clean home?

If you can't meet the animal's needs for any of these reasons, don't get a cat. Millions of animals die in shelters every year because people did not take the time to ask themselves a few basic questions. A pet is not something that should be considered disposable. Like adopting a child, adopting a pet should be for life.

Common Breeds of Cats

When you start looking for a cat, the first thing you may wonder is what breed to get. Realistically, unlike dogs, you don't find many officially purebred cats at animal shelters. However, you do run across the acronyms DSH and DLH a lot. These acronyms stand for "domestic short hair" and "domestic long hair," respectively. Most cats of, shall we say, uncertain ancestry are lumped into these rather general "breed categories."

The "ordinary house cat" is most often a domestic short hair. These mixed-breed (sometimes called "random bred") cats are by far the most popular cats in American homes. Domestic longhaired cats may come in a variety of fur lengths, which may require a bit more maintenance than their short-coated counterparts.

The named breeds you are most likely to encounter at a shelter are Persians, Siamese, Maine Coons, and very occasionally more unusual breeds like Abyssinians. However, because the distinguishing features of cat breeds can be quite minute, at a shelter, you may see any number of breed names used to describe a cat. For example, a longhaired cat might be called a domestic long hair (DLH), Himalayan, Balinese, Persian, or Maine Coon, whether or not it has any vestige of "purebred" cat in it.

Persian cats are often confused with other longhaired cats by people who aren't familiar with them. Not every longhaired cat is a Persian. A true Persian cat has fur that is longer than any other breed. Because of this long hair, they require a tremendous amount of maintenance to keep the cat from becoming a matted mess. Persians are stocky cats with small ears. Although most people are more familiar with "extreme" Persians, which have the distinctive "pushed in" face, "traditional" Persians have a less flattened look with a more prominent nose.

Maine Coon cats are large cats with heavy, silky coats. They most commonly have a brown tabby coat pattern. Considering it is so large, a Maine Coon cat often has a very small voice. This dainty meow is in sharp contrast to the Siamese, which is probably the most vocal cat you will encounter. If you like quiet kitties, you might not enjoy life with a Siamese, since they always have something to say.

Siamese are shorthaired cats that are easily recognized by their "pointed" coat pattern. A cat that looks like a longhaired Siamese is actually a different breed called a Balinese. Many people confuse the Balinese with the Himalayan, which is actually a cross between a Siamese and a Persian. Technically, in the cat fancier world, a Himalayan is just a Persian with a pointed coat pattern.

Again, an estimated 95% of cats have no traceable ancestry. A vocal cat is not necessarily a Siamese (even though she may sound like one). No matter what cat you get, the bottom line is that the lowliest "mutt kitty" needs just as much care and love as the most expensive purebred.

Cat Coloring

To many people, the term "tabby" is almost synonymous with the word "cat." (Hence the title of this book.) Some people think of the standard "domestic short hair" cat as a tabby.

However, the term tabby actually doesn't refer to a breed of cat, but rather a fur pattern. If your cat has fur with spots, stripes, or whorls and the distinctive M on his forehead, he's a tabby. Four different tabby patterns exist. The tabby stripes that many people refer to as "tiger stripes" actually are the pattern found in a "mackerel" tabby, which is the most common variety. A "classic" tabby has a whirling pattern like marble cake. A spotted tabby has spots on his sides, and a "ticked" tabby actually doesn't have stripes or spots at all.

On any tabby, the individual hairs have bands of color. This banding pattern is called "agouti" and ticked tabbies have agouti hairs. Many Abyssinian cats are ticked tabbies, and the agouti hair is what causes their fur to seem to shimmer in the light.

Tabbies also come in a number of different colors: brown, blue (the cat fancier term for gray), red (the term for orange), cream, and silver. Of course, not all cats are tabbies. Solid color cats exist as well. They may be black, gray, blue (a slate gray color), and white. The feline gene for solid color is recessive, so many cats that appear to be a solid color actually may have tabby markings if you look closely in the light. Don't be surprised to see evidence of extremely subtle tabby stripes on your black cat when he's lying around in the sun. Black and white cats are often called "tuxedos" since they often look like they are dressed in formal attire.

Cats that have multiple patches of colors are generally tortoise shell, patched tabby, or calico. Patched tabbies have two separate colors of tabby on the same cat. For example, a "blue patched tabby" has patches of blue tabby and patches of cream tabby. A calico cat has separate solid blocks of red (i.e., orange), black, and white. A tortoiseshell or "tortie," on the other hand, mingles the colors together.

Points are another variety of feline coat pattern. If the cat has darker fur on its face, paws, and tail, it's considered a "pointed" cat. Although you find this pattern in Siamese cats, many other breeds and non-purebred cats also have points. In other words, just because your cat has points, that doesn't mean he is a purebred.

Kitten or Cat?

When you are considering getting a cat, one of your first decisions is whether to get a kitten or an adult cat. Shelters are invariably full of both kittens and cats, so except for very rare occasions, you can find a kitten if you want one.

Kittens are one of life's most adorable creatures. Who among us can observe a kitten playfully scampering around the floor and not even crack a smile? Of course, all that adorable playfulness comes at a price. The old saying about "curiosity killed the cat" goes double for kittens. They explore, play, and get into anything they can get their fuzzy little selves near.

If you get a kitten, you need to take steps to "kitten proof" your house. If the kitten can get into something, he will. Your job as caretaker is to make sure he doesn't get hurt. So to avoid feline disaster, you may have to do things like install cabinet locks, secure cords, and/or remove glassware and other breakables from places the kitten can access. Remember that, unlike a small child, kittens are incredibly agile little things and can jump up to places far higher than you might think.

If you get a kitten you also will need to devote more time to supervising the youngster's activities to keep him out of trouble. If you have small children, you also should think twice before getting a kitten. Kittens are tiny and can easily be hurt by children or vice versa. If you have elderly people or anyone who has trouble walking living in your household, a tiny kitten can cause a lot of problems if he is zooming around getting underfoot everywhere.

Adopting an adult cat avoids some of the pitfalls of adopting a kitten. With an adult cat, you can evaluate his personality far more easily. Kittens are still forming their personalities and many are hard to distinguish from one another. However, with an adult cat, you'll know from the outset if he's shy and aloof, or outgoing and friendly.

Depending on why the cat has been brought to the shelter, yes, it is possible that he may have been brought in because of a behavior problem. If so, the shelter should note it on the paperwork. However, many times, there's just no way to know what went on in the cat's "previous life," and many cats seem to know that they have been rescued and bond strongly with their owners.

Kitten Myths

Everybody loves kittens. Without a doubt, they're invariably adorable. However, there seems to be a lot of misinformation surrounding them. Here is a list of a few myths that require debunking:

Myth: Kittens can be weaned at 4 weeks.

Fact: If your cat has had kittens, do not try to sell, give away, or bring them to a shelter until they are at least 7–8 weeks old. If you don't know how old they are, weigh them. A kitten should weigh at least two pounds before it is taken away from its mother. Young kittens do not have fully developed immune systems yet, so taking them away from Mom too early makes them vulnerable to disease. So WAIT until they are old enough. The new owners, whether the shelter or a new "parent," do not want to deal with the heartbreak of a sick or dying kitten. And once the kittens are weaned, get the mother cat fixed. There are way, way too many unwanted kittens in the world that are being euthanized every day.

Myth: A 6-week-old kitten is ready to come home with me.

Fact: The corollary to myth #1 is that if you decide to get a kitten, don't get one that is less than 7 or 8 weeks old. You don't want a sick kitten. Also be sure to take the kitten to a veterinarian.

Myth: It doesn't matter who gives me a free kitten because it was free.

Fact: Don't get a kitten or cat from anyone who won't let you see its prior living conditions or seems reluctant to answer your questions about the kitten.

Myth: The littlest/sickest kitten needs me the most.

Fact: Don't select a kitten that has diarrhea, looks weak or thin, is sneezing, or has runny eyes. As mentioned, kittens are susceptible to many diseases and it may have an upper respiratory infection or worse. Contrary to popular belief, outdoor cats are especially at risk for a number of feline diseases for which there are NO vaccines and NO cures.

The more you learn the facts about kittens and cats the better pet owner you will be!

Should You Get a Male or Female Cat?

Few things are as adorable as a tiny kitty tripping all over herself and pouncing on imaginary carpet interlopers. Pretty much every kitten is cute, but they'll be cats for a lot longer than they'll be kittens. Before you become completely smitten with the first cuddly ball of fur you meet, you should consider a basic question. Do you want a male or a female cat?

Each gender has pros and cons associated with it. Although feline personalities vary widely, male cats are often more friendly than female cats. Many male cats have a cuddly "lap cat" personality. Female cats are often more cautious and may take longer to trust you. However, once you've proven your worth, they too can be very affectionate. Male cats are often significantly larger than female cats. But if you want a calico cat, you pretty much have to get a female.

The main disadvantage of male cats is that they "spray." If you see a male cat with his tail straight up in the air backing toward a wall, he's probably spraying it with urine. The resulting horrible smell will be your next clue. However, in most cases, spraying isn't a problem if you get the cat neutered at a young age. (Talk to your veterinarian for more advice on when to have your cat neutered.) If you adopt a cat from a shelter, he may already be neutered or they will require that you get the cat fixed before you can adopt him.

Although sometimes more aloof, female cats are far less likely to spray. However, if you don't get the cat fixed, she may become a mother long before you might expect. Cats can have a litter of kittens before their first birthday, so again, talk to your vet about getting the cat spayed. Unspayed females also "vocalize" (read: yowl loudly) when they come into heat, which is yet another reason to get that cute little kitten spayed as soon as the vet recommends.

Although opinions differ, some people say that if you already have a cat, you may want to get one of the opposite sex. On the other hand, I introduced a female kitten into our household, which already had an older female cat, and we haven't had problems.

Female cats are often better mousers than males. Cats of either gender that are "fixed" are better mousers than those that are intact because they think about hunting and not finding a mate. Of course, mousing ability depends a lot more on the cat's personality than the sex of the cat. I have two female cats and they are both completely clueless mousers.

The bottom line is that cats are individuals. Both female and male cats can make wonderful companions. When you are tempted by that adorable kitten, remember he or she will be around for 10 or 15 years, so be sure you are prepared to make that type of commitment to a new pet.

Acquiring a Cat

Now that you've made your decision to adopt and pondered all the various shapes, colors, and sizes of cats you may encounter, it's time to begin looking for your new feline.

When you decide you want a cat, these are your main options:

1. Get a cat from a pet store.
2. Get a cat from a responsible (show) breeder.
3. Get a "free" cat from an ad in the paper or that wanders onto your property.
4. Get a cat from a shelter or breed rescue.

Of course, this book is about adoption and rescue, so option number four is the one I hope you will choose. I also discuss a few issues surrounding option three, since many people end up owning "free" cats this way.

Visiting animal shelters can be both fun and stressful. Depending on the shelter, you may suddenly find yourself confronted with dozens, even hundreds of potential feline companions. You may experience powerful emotions, including confusion, indecision, and even a little anger. Seeing all those wonderful animals that need homes makes you wonder how people could be so heartless.

At times like this, remember that you are trying to do your part. By choosing to adopt a shelter critter, you really are making the world a little more humane and giving one special cat a great life. Remember that the nominal fee you pay to the shelter means more than you realize. Take the word of a former shelter volunteer: every adoption is a triumph for the folks who keep those cats healthy and find them good homes!

You can also reduce your stress level by being prepared. Always listen to your gut feelings, and your heart, when choosing any pet. Looks aren't everything and any happy, healthy, well-socialized cat can make a great companion.

If you don't have a good feeling about the shelter, the staff, or the animals, walk away. In literally every part of the country, and in even the most remote areas, there are always plenty of cats available for adoption. You can even start your search online at sites like:

http://www.petfinder.com or

http://www.pets911.com

In this chapter, I cover all the adoption basics, including what to look for in a rescue group or shelter, the truth about "free" cats, and what to do with that stray you've been feeding.

Ready? Let's go find your new feline friend!

Adopting from a Shelter

As the owner of two "mutt tabbies," I'm not exactly a purist when it comes to cats. Even if you want a purebred cat, it's possible that you can find one at an animal shelter, particularly if you are willing to wait. Although you may not get paperwork that proves a cat is a particular breed, you probably can get a cat that looks a lot like a Persian, a Siamese, or almost any other breed of cat.

When you adopt a cat from an animal shelter, you often receive a package that contains food and coupons, a collar, an identification tag, a handbook explaining how to care for your new pet, and a free health exam at a local veterinarian.

Most shelters give incoming cats a full set of shots and wormer. The cat also is evaluated for temperament, so ask a lot of questions. Shelter staff often have been interacting with the cat for quite some time, so they can give you good insights into her personality.

After you take the cat to a veterinarian, if they find a health problem that was missed at the shelter, virtually all shelters let you return the animal. If you and the cat are incompatible for some reason, most shelters, again, will let you return the cat.

In many cases, the animal shelter will follow up with you to make sure you and your cat are doing okay and to help with advice if you are having problems with any unexpected behaviors.

Adopting from Rescue

Many people are under the impression that the only way to get a cat is to go to a pet store, breeder, or animal shelter. However, this is not true. Many rescue groups exist that aren't related to a shelter. Volunteers foster needy cats in their homes and then adopt them out. Sometimes they are affiliated with breed fanciers, but not always. As I said, I got my cat Alia from a rescue that was affiliated with the county animal shelters. Alia never saw the inside of a shelter, and I never went into one to get her.

If you are looking for a particular breed of cat, a shelter may or may not have the breed you want at the time you want to get a cat. Although many animal shelters will put your name on a list and contact you when a particular breed comes in, waiting for the right cat to arrive may take a while. Purebred rescue groups are another option.

Although they aren't as organized as those for dogs, a few cat rescue groups do exist and cats whose owners can't keep them often get a second chance through a rescue group that is dedicated to saving a particular breed.

Rescues can be a wonderful source of healthy, well-mannered, spayed or neutered pets for your family. In some cases, the rescue may be just one person who loves and is knowledgeable about a particular breed. Other groups may be involved with national breed clubs or larger rescue networks. In any case, a reputable rescue can be a tremendous source of advice and information about a breed.

So now you've decided to save a life and adopt a cat through rescue. Finding a rescue club for your favorite breed is your next challenge. A good first step is to call your animal shelter. Because shelters often do work with many rescues, they may be able to give you a contact number. If they don't have one, you also can try doing some research on the Internet. Type in the name of the breed and the word "rescue" and you should find a few.

The Darker Side of Rescue

Although rescues may sound like a great option, you should know that not all "rescues" are legitimate. The darker side of rescue is that not all groups who claim to be "rescuing" animals out of shelters really are.

Many so-called rescue groups are just fronts for backyard breeders, or worse. Instead of paying big money for purebred animals, these "rescues" just pluck them out of shelters for a few bucks. Instead of saving animals, they are contributing to pet overpopulation by breeding even more animals to make some quick cash. In fact, sadly some shelters won't deal with rescues at all for this reason.

Legitimate rescues often have expert-level knowledge of the breed and can provide the veterinary care, training, socialization, screening, and information necessary to make successful placements. If you are thinking of getting a cat through rescue, ask a LOT of questions of the rescue group. They should give you complete and thorough answers.

If any animals on their premises aren't spayed or neutered, ask why. Look around the facility. If it looks (or smells) like a backyard breeder, it probably is. As when visiting and evaluating a shelter, trust your instincts. Be very suspicious, and if you get a bad feeling from the person or their facility, find a different rescue.

Fly By Night Kitties

There's a time and a place for everything. When you need food, you go to the grocery store. When you want to find a mean deal on household items, you head for a flea market. Neither of these places are good places to get your next cat, however.

It may seem innocuous enough to "adopt" that adorable kitten in the parking lot, but think about what you are doing. Grocers put the candy in the checkout aisle for the same reason people give away puppies and kittens in parking lots. They're hoping for an impulse purchase. However, getting a cat on a whim is a big mistake. And it's why an estimated 50% of the animals you see being given away in parking lots and flea markets end up at animal shelters.

When you get a pet from someone in a parking lot, you have no idea what conditions that animal has been living in. The animal may be ill or housed in squalid conditions. It may be a kitten from a family pet, or maybe not. Even if the person giving away animals says they've vaccinated the animal, you rarely, if ever, get any proof.

Realize that the person will be gone tomorrow, so if there's a problem, you have no recourse. Young kittens are susceptible to disease and could be infected with such diseases as feline leukemia, respiratory diseases, or feline panleukopenia (a.k.a. feline distemper). When you take that cute little critter home, you expose your own animals to these contagious diseases as well.

Reputable rescues and shelters vaccinate all animals and keep their living quarters clean and disinfected. "Free kittens" are not such a bargain when you consider vet bills. You'll have to take the kitten to the veterinarian to get her vaccinated, at the very least. If the animal is already sick, you may have to spend a lot of money in medical care or even have it euthanized. (Unfortunately, vets see this type of scenario far too often.)

Talk to reputable rescues and shelters about their policies. If you have problems or concerns, you want to deal with a shelter or rescue that will be there tomorrow to help you.

Finders Keepers

Another way people tend to acquire "free" cats is by finding them. (Or more accurately, the cat finds you.) A lot of confusion surrounds the concept of pet ownership. People often deny ownership of pets that have been living on their property for years. Conversely, just because you find an animal, that does not make it yours.

The laws are reasonably clear: the "owner" of an animal is generally described as the person who owns, keeps, harbors, possesses, has custodial care of, or acts as caretaker. That means the stray cat you've been feeding for the last 6 months is your cat. And as the owner, you may be held liable for any damages that animal causes to someone else's home or property.

The problem with pets is that unlike a lawn mower or other personal property, an animal can wander off. Don't assume that a pet you find has been "abandoned" or "dumped," even if you live out in the country. An owner may be frantically searching for the animal. It's your responsibility to report any animals you find to the local authorities or animal shelter.

If you report the animal and make an honest attempt to find the owner, but no one comes forward, generally, you become the owner by default if you keep the animal on your property. Check the local laws in your area, but before you adopt an animal in this way, make sure you understand your legal rights.

A Kitten for Christmas?

Almost every year, some advertising executive has a great idea to run a TV commercial that includes an adorable kitten with a big red bow around his neck sitting under the Christmas tree. However, I'd like to suggest that you avoid the temptation to give a kitten as a gift.

Most people are extremely busy over the holidays and unfortunately, the sad reality is that some of those Christmas kittens end up at shelters in January. Think long and hard before you decide to give anyone a pet as a gift. Be honest with yourself and consider your situation.

Is the nature of your job such that you have more or less time over the holidays? If you work in retail, for example, you may have a lot less time. But if you are a teacher, you might have some time off.

Any pet, but especially a baby like a kitten needs a lot of extra attention when you first bring it home. The new furry member of your household should be a priority—remember that he may be a member of your household for the next 15 years. It's also important for everybody to learn the home routine. It's not fair to the kitten if you won't be able to spend any time with her during the chaotic holiday season.

Kittens get into everything and need to be watched constantly. Ornaments, wires, lights, tinsel, and other holiday paraphernalia can be dangerous to a curious young pet. It's a lot easier to deal with a new kitten after the decorations have been put away.

With all these caveats in mind, it's not always a terrible idea for people to get pets over the holidays. For example, those spending the holiday season alone may benefit from the company of a new furry friend. People without kids or who are retired with extra time available may do well sharing the season with a new cat.

However, you really should never give a cat (or any other pet) to someone who is not expecting it. Getting a pet should be a family decision (even if your family is just you). Shelters are filled with furry gifts that were "returned." A cat is never a good surprise, since the recipient may not be able to take on the financial and personal responsibility for another living creature for the next 15 years. Not to mention the fact that choosing a pet is a very personal decision. It's not one that should be made for someone else.

If the latest adorable kitten commercial has tempted you to get a cat, talk about it with your family. Look at it as an educational opportunity. Wrap presents such as a collar, leash, and a book on pet care (like this one). Then visit an animal shelter or rescue after the holidays, so everyone can pick out the new family friend together.

TROI

The Feline Early Warning System

Our cats are rather pathetic mousers. They like to chase mice, but they don't dispatch them. Our offices are downstairs, and sometimes we'll hear great thundering noises from above as the feline team chase a mouse around. It sounds different than their usual play romping, which also is loud, but perhaps not quite as insistent.

Troi, the small brown tabby huntress, figured out long ago that if you kill the mouse, the game is over. Since she is well fed, she's not into mousing for the food; she's into it for the sport. In fact, we have occasionally found Troi sitting face to face with an exhausted mouse, waiting for it to get a second wind so she can chase it some more. (In this situation, we take pity on the mouse and return him to the great outdoors.)

Having mice in your house is not a good thing, and at some point, we discovered that the mice tend to travel under the stove behind the drawer. Since our cats won't hunt, we set mousetraps back there. If a mouse gets inside the house, the cats find and chase it. Eventually the mouse runs behind the stove and encounters the traps. The mouse rarely survives the journey behind the stove.

So this morning, when we found Troi staring at the stove, we knew exactly what was behind the drawer. We have a rodent control system that works. The cats aren't completely useless. We have a feline early warning system to tell us when it's time to check the traps.

Bringing Your Cat Home

As with people, part of an animal's emotional makeup is based on past experiences. Sometimes you adopt a cat that came from a wonderful home, but sometimes a cat has had a "checkered past."

No matter what happened before, your new adopted pet has no way of knowing what the rules are at your house. However, with a little understanding and TLC, you can help your new kitty feel safe, comfortable, and part of the family.

The First Days

When you bring your new kitten or cat home, you should be prepared. If you spend some time in the pet section of your favorite store or start perusing pet catalogs, you'll quickly see that you could spend a small fortune on your new furry friend if you're not careful. So here's a list of the basics you need for your new cat:

Essential Cat Supplies

Here is a list of the basics you need for your new kitty:

Bowls. You need at least one bowl for water and one for food. Stainless steel bowls are easy to clean and don't get scratched easily. Scratches in plastic can harbor germs. Plus, some cats have been known to play with their food or water. If your cat has a predisposition to play with his tableware, you also might want to consider a weighted bowl, so she doesn't throw food or water everywhere. (We had to make a device for our kitty auto-waterer to keep it in place because our cat Alia enjoyed sliding it down our tile hallway; what a mess!)

Food. Consult with your veterinarian on recommended food for your cat. Kittens, older cats, and cats with various health issues may require special foods.

A bed. Cats love having snuggly places to snooze. If you want to encourage your cat not to sleep on your bed or other furniture, get her one of her own.

A kitty carrier. These look like small versions of the "sky kennels" you see for dogs. It is used to hold your cat for trips to the vet or other destinations. A loose cat wandering around your car is not a good idea.

Scratching post, board, or "kitty tree." Scratching the furniture is one of the most common complaints cat owners have. If you teach your cat to use the tree, she won't use the couch. You do need the tree or scratching device for this plan to work though.

Toys. Your cat's age and athletic abilities determine the best toys for her. Some cats love chasing things attached to a string. Others are more "paw-centric" and love batting balls around the room. Experiment with a few inexpensive toys first and see what goes over well before investing in anything elaborate.

A collar and ID. A collar with identification is *the most* important thing you can buy for your cat. I'll be blunt: not keeping identification on any pet is stupid and irresponsible. No good reason exists for your cat to be without a collar and ID, ever. Contrary to popular belief, cat collars are safe. They have a quick-release and all the old horror stories about cats getting caught on fence posts are blown way out of proportion.

Far more cats die from ***not*** wearing a collar and ID than from wearing one.

A leash and harness. If you travel with your cat, it's handy to have a harness and leash just in case. Situations arise where the cat isn't in the carrier, so it can be helpful to have her on a leash. Cats can leap out of your arms with astonishing speed. If she's on a leash, she won't be able to run away.

It's good to get your shopping done before you get the cat, but she will forgive you if everything isn't just "perfect" before you bring her home. Just be sure to get the ID on the cat ASAP. (After all, you just adopted the cat from a shelter; do you really want her to end up back there?)

Indoor Cat Happiness

It's a mistake to think that it's "mean" to keep your cat inside. When you get a kitten, if you keep her inside, it's unlikely she will be interested in the great outdoors later in life. I've met plenty of indoor-only cats who seem to be just as happy as any other cat. My cats, for example, don't seem to be deprived by remaining indoors. It has undoubtedly increased their life span, given the number of coyotes and owls in our neck of the woods. One of my cats is 14 years old, which is far older than the average life span of an outdoor cat.

The biggest key to keeping an indoor cat happy is to pay attention to her. If you keep her environment interesting with toys and give her lots of attention, she'll be just as happy (or happier) than a cat that gets to go outdoors, but rarely interacts with her family.

Realistically, cats sleep a lot, so you need to provide safe areas where the feline can get away from it all and take a nap. A kitty bed strategically placed near a window makes a fine place for some serious snoring in the sun. Kitty trees or condos can be great relaxation spots as well. We made our own kitty tree out of some pieces of downed wood, scrap carpet, and sisal rope. The whole thing probably cost about $10 and the cats love it.

If you have more than one cat, they can help keep each other entertained. Our cats run around and chase each other almost every morning, zooming around the room and up and down the kitty tree. If you only have one cat, you do need to make time to play with her every day, so she gets enough exercise to remain healthy. Toys don't have to be expensive either. It's easy to amuse a cat simply by dragging a piece of crumpled up paper tied to an old shoelace. Our cats also are fond of paper bags and boxes.

If you have an indoor cat, it's particularly important to keep the litter box clean, since the cat can't use the great outdoors as an alternate lavatory. You also should keep a collar and ID on her, in case she accidentally does get outside. You or people visiting your house can leave doors or windows open. Unfortunately, shelters are overflowing with cats that "got lost," and the return rate statistics are dismal because so few people put collars on cats. A standard "quick-release" collar equipped with an ID tag is a simple and safe way to ensure your cat is returned to you.

Indoor cats don't have to be miserable cats. In fact, they often live longer, healthier, and happier lives than indoor–outdoor kitties. With a little consideration on your part, your cat can enjoy life in the comfort of your home.

Spaying and Neutering

After you adopt a kitten or cat, you may need to get it spayed or neutered. A lot of myths surround the subject of spaying and neutering pets, and probably the biggest myth is that getting an animal altered is bad for the animal. This is simply not true.

When a female cat is spayed, she can't get uterine or ovarian cancer and the possibility that she'll get breast cancer is greatly reduced. Another myth is that it's good to let a cat have one litter before getting her spayed. Medical research indicates the opposite: females that are spayed before their first heat cycle are typically healthier. Plus, you no longer have to endure the loud yowling "love songs" of a female cat in heat.

If you have a male cat, neutering is a simple surgery that will make life with your cat a lot better. Neutered cats are far less likely to spray and they lose the urge to fight with other cats. So you won't have all those expensive trips to the vet to get abscesses drained. They also can't get testicular cancer, since, well, the testicles are no longer there. As with female cats, neutered cats also have a lowered risk for mammary cancer.

Another pervasive myth is that spaying or neutering makes a cat "fat and lazy." However, the only thing that will make your cat fat and lazy is if you feed her too much or don't give her enough exercise. Many people also think that spaying is expensive. But it doesn't have to be.

Many vets offer low-cost spay/neuter services and animal shelters often have cost-assistance programs as well. All you have to do is call. Spaying is a one-time cost that is minuscule when compared to the cost of providing care for a mother and a litter (or litters!) of kittens.

Plus, that "just one litter" contributes to the problem of pet overpopulation. Even if you find homes for the kittens, those cats produce kittens and the problem grows exponentially and quickly.

In six years, one female cat and her offspring can be the source of literally thousands of cats. There really aren't enough homes for them all. So, you should get your cat spayed or neutered not just because it's good for the cat, but also because it's the right thing to do.

Early Age Spay/Neuter

As I said, because of the health and behavior benefits, spaying or neutering is one of the most important things you can do for your cat. However, when you get a new kitten, that magic age of 5 or 6 months can really sneak up on you. Suddenly your formerly adorable kitty is acting a whole lot different as he or she starts sniffing around for a date. Then when you aren't looking, your feline teenager gets pregnant or starts running around yowling and annoying the neighborhood. Now you have big problems.

One way to avoid these situations is to get your kitten spayed or neutered earlier than the traditional 6 months. Getting an animal fixed at anywhere from 7 to 16 weeks of age is termed "early age spay/neuter." Although still sometimes considered "controversial" in the veterinary community, early age spay/neuter now has more than 10 years of research and published studies to recommend it. Although in the past there were concerns about the future health of the animal or the danger of the surgery, the research indicates that puppies and kittens suffer no medical or behavioral side effects.

In fact, the American Veterinary Medical Association has endorsed early age spay/neuter. They say, "... AVMA supports the concept of early (8 to 16 weeks of age) ovariohysterectomies and gonadectomies in dogs and cats, in an effort to stem the overpopulation problem in these species." The procedure also is endorsed by The Humane Society of the United States, The American Kennel Club, The American Humane Association, Davis University School of Veterinary Medicine, Cornell University School of Veterinary Medicine, Pacific Coast SPCA, The Good Neighbor Animal Alliance Center, K9 Haven, Alley Cat Allies, and many more.

Veterinarians differ in their opinions of the benefits of early age spay/neuter, so ask. Many vets say that some of the problems they see can be prevented if the animal is altered before puberty. As I pointed out, spaying a female cat before her first heat cycle has a number of health benefits. Plus, male cats that come into vet clinics with abscesses, gunshot wounds, prostate problems, and testicular cancer almost invariably haven't been neutered.

It's tragic that so many of these animals die unnecessarily from problems that could be prevented by spaying or neutering. If you think you "can't afford" to get your pet fixed, think about the long-term medical costs of not getting your cat fixed.

TROI

The Chief Mouse Warden

The other day, I was sitting in the kitchen, minding my own business, reading the newspaper. Troi, the fat cat, was staring at me. She stares at me regularly within two hours of her feeding times. Sometimes she has a tiny kitty hunger pang and can't contain herself anymore, so she whines. These cries of starvation are not met with sympathy or enthusiasm from me.

In any case, I was reading and Troi was staring and starving (at least in her mind). Troi was not, however, tending to her feline duty as chief mouse warden. It was quiet with all that reading and staring, and suddenly there was a loud "THWAP" sound. I leaped out of my chair and looked down at Troi. She looked at the kitchen stove because the big noise seemed to have come from that direction.

And then I knew what the noise was. A mousetrap. (Eww!)

For some reason, the area behind the drawer of the stove is the mouse superhighway. I don't know how they get inside, but as noted, that's inevitably where mice meet their doom. At our house, we all have our responsibilities. Removing slow rodents from traps is not one of mine, so I wrote my husband James a note and told him that it was time to pull out the stove drawer and check the trap.

As I went downstairs to go to work, I realized that the chief mouse warden should be fired. Any cat that doesn't notice a mouse less than 6 feet away is a disgrace to felinekind.

Adjusting to the Family

In many cases, you won't have much information about your adopted feline's background, so when making family introductions you may be flying blind because you have no past experience to go on.

You've probably met cats who seem basically unfazed by anything, and ones that are startled by the slightest noise. If the cat is still young, you have a golden opportunity to expose her to new experiences (a process called "socialization") to help her become a happy, well-adjusted pet.

As far as your adopted cat is concerned, "family" isn't just you and your spouse, partner, children, and even elderly parents who live with you. It includes all the other animals in your household, whether they are dogs or guinea pigs!

If people other than your immediate family enter your home regularly, such as a health care worker, household help, or dog walker, be sure to take them into account as well. You need to make sure everyone understands their role in your cat's life (and vice versa).

To help make adjusting to the family easier for everyone, let's look at some of the most common scenarios you will face as you introduce your cat to her new family.

The New Kitten

When you bring home a new kitten, odds are that everyone in your house will be very excited about the new addition to the family. But you should remember that your kitten is very tiny and to her, you are very huge. For many kittens dealing with so many gigantic humans, loud noises, and unfamiliar smells can be overwhelming. Those first hours at the new homestead can be traumatic, so take a few steps to help her adjust.

Before you bring home your new cat or kitten, prepare a confined area for her to stay. Set up a bed and her litter box in there, along with a few toys. Keeping her in a spare bedroom or bathroom for a few nights makes it easier for her to adjust to the new space gradually. (Again, to a little kitten, your bathroom may seem like a vast new frontier.)

When you bring your kitten into your house, also make sure you choose a time when the house is quiet. If you have another cat at home, keep the existing cat and the new cat separated for a few days so that they can get used to each other's scent.

After the new cat has adjusted somewhat, let the two meet. They may hiss at one another or one may run away. If they should get into a fight, squirt them with water and confine one or both of them and try again later. If you have dogs or young children, the same rules apply. Make sure to introduce them to the new cat slowly under close supervision. Kids and canines alike should understand that the new cat is not a toy. Never let either one of them tease or chase the cat.

Remember that a kitten is just a baby; as a good parent you should be there to help her cope with new experiences. When the going gets tough, pick her up out of harm's way to help her feel secure.

Feline and Canine Cohabitation

When I worked at an animal shelter, I was often asked whether or not a cat "gets along" with dogs or if a certain dog "gets along" with cats. However, a better question is: "Can this dog be trained to get along with cats?" Most dogs will chase virtually any moving object. Carnivores have an instinctive behavior referred to as "prey drive." If something runs, the dog thinks, "must be prey" and chases. That includes cats. Your job as an owner is to tell the dog that this particular object should not be chased.

If you train the dog, the cat will feel safe and will "get along" with it. At our house, for example, both dogs and cats know that in any situation, the cat wins and the dog is going to get in trouble if he "messes with the cat."

With the exception of a few dogs with a really strong prey drive, almost any dog can be trained to get along with the cats in your house. To get started, all you need is a leash and a baby gate or piece of wood to block off a doorway.

If your dog already knows basic commands such as "leave it" or "down" you may not even need a leash. If you see the dog chase the cat, tell him "no cat" and give him a "down" command. Praise him if he complies. If your dog doesn't comply, put a leash on him and let him drag it around, so the next time he goes after the cat you can step on the end of the leash and stop him. When he turns to look at you, give him the "no cat" and "down" commands. Reinforce the good behavior with lots of praise.

The baby gate is more for the cat than the dog. It lets you block off an area so the cat can get away from the dog to a safe place. Your cat will appreciate other dog-free areas such as a feeding place that's up high or away from nasty canine snouts. Some people put a kitty door into a closet so their cats can have a private area for litter box and feeding times.

With a little bit of effort on your part acting as intermediary, it's easy to live a peaceful existence with both canines and felines.

Kids and Pets

When you get a pet, you need to step back and evaluate your kids' attitude toward animals. Many children have never had any guidelines as to the proper rules for dealing with animals. Some kids run up to animals recklessly and others shy away in fear when they encounter one. Learning respect for animals should be a big part of growing up, but the increasing number of bite incidents is clear evidence that parents aren't telling kids what they need to know.

Start teaching your kids about animals at an early age. Show them how to listen and learn about their animal compatriots by watching critters from a distance at first. Point out birds in the trees or dogs in the neighbor's yard and discuss the animal's behaviors.

Visit zoos, shelters, ranches, and other places where animals are in a controlled setting. Show your kids how to approach animals in non-threatening ways and get animal-related books from the library to educate your kids on the roles animals play in our lives.

Teach your children to be gentle. You might show them how to stroke an animal gently on a stuffed animal first, and then graduate to a friend's pet that you know is very gentle. Be sure to teach your child not to chase or hit any animal. Studies show that cruelty to animals is frequently linked to human violence and abuse. A kid that is taught to care about animals learns that animals and people are living things that should not be treated violently.

When you are researching getting a pet, have your child help you research breeds and read about pet care. When you go to look for your new cat or kitten, explain that owning an animal is a lifetime commitment and point out that animals should not be treated as disposable "throw away" toys.

Also accept the fact that if your child is 10 now, and a cat lives to be 15, it may be just you and that feline sharing his senior years. Show your kids the importance of having the pet as a family member, but don't expect small children to take full responsibility for caring for an animal.

Getting a pet is a fantastic opportunity for education. Kids that have been taught to respect animals learn to look at the world around them in a more humane, caring way. And who wouldn't want that for their kids?

Keeping Track of the Cat

A sad reality is that few cats that get lost are ever returned to their owners. One study showed only two percent of cats that end up in shelters are reunited with their families. My cats wear collars and tags, and as I've written before, a mere $2 spent on a collar and tag can get your cat home again. Some people seem to think that collars are somehow "dangerous" (even though quick-release collars have been around for years). But if you are really against putting a collar on Fluffy, you have another option: microchipping. A microchip is about the size of a grain of rice and contains a transponder that can be read by a microchip reader that is scanned over the animal's body.

Most vets offer microchipping of companion pets, and in many areas of the country, shelters microchip every animal they adopt because a microchip increases return to owner rates dramatically. One shelter director in Washington I talked to many years ago called microchipping "the best thing we've ever done."

Although the technology has been around for ages, microchipping does have a few drawbacks. The first is that it's not a visible form of identification. All shelters have been donated "universal" scanners, and shelter staffs are supposed to scan every animal they receive. If the scanner finds a signal, it means there's a microchip and an owner out there somewhere. The shelter then calls the microchip company, which has a database of records that match up the pet with the owner.

Unfortunately, the process doesn't always result in joyful happy endings and rainbows. User error, microchip, and database issues can keep Fluffy from making it home. Some shelter staff either don't scan animals correctly or don't do it at all. Because some shelters only hold strays for a short period of time, a pet can be either adopted or euthanized before the owner contacts the shelter.

The other problem may be the chip itself. In the U.S., two primary chip manufacturers have existed for years. Both AVID and Home Again microchips use a frequency of 125kHz (FDX-A). Unfortunately, a large pet hospital called Banfield that operates in PetSmart stores for a time sold chips that work at 134.2kHz (ISO FDX-B). Although this chip frequency is widely used outside the U.S., the bad news is that the "universal" scanners used in most U.S. shelters couldn't read the chips. Banfield subsequently stopped selling the chips and Home Again announced that it has a scanner that can read the 134.2kHz chips, but of course some shelters still don't have them.

Finally, the owner information registered with the microchip company needs to be up to date. A database is only as good as the data contained in it. The information may be registered to the veterinarian who inserted the chip or to the owner. If the owner moves, and especially if the owner moves more than once, it can become difficult to match up the pet with the owner. Before you microchip your pet, find out what chips are used in your area and keep your information up to date in the database.

Although microchips are a great option, they aren't a substitute for a collar and tags in my opinion. Many people are lazy. If they see a tag, they know the cat has an owner and can call easily. Sure, get your pet a microchip, but also spend the $2 on a collar and tags, so the lazy guy can call you too.

TROI

Cross-Species Communication

Cat and dog interactions are a strange thing. I suspect that in the wild, canines and felines would never be caught fraternizing in the same area of the tundra or wilderness. It just isn't done.

But when you live with four dogs and two cats you get to see a lot of cross-species communication. We're not exactly sure what Cami, the Samoyed mix, is trying to do or say with Troi, the tubby tabby, but I'm not sure it's good. As a dog with a lot of Samoyed in her, Cami has perfected what Samoyed owners refer to as the "bossy nose poke."

In fact, mere moments ago, Cami came over to my chair, sat down purposefully, bestowed a particularly adorable smile upon me, and poked my arm. This sequence of events generally means, "Look! I'm cute! It's after 6; go feed me now." (Or something along those lines.) As a human pokee, I either acquiesce to her demanding nature, or continue writing. (One would note I'm still typing and Cami is now lying on the floor with her back to me, pouting.)

I often wonder what Cami is trying to communicate to Troi when she gives her a bossy nose poke. I'm not sure Troi gets it either. As a bold, small cat who has been around dogs almost all her life, Troi has no fear of canines. She walks between their feet, rubs up on their legs, plays with their tails, and sometimes even curls up and sleeps with them.

Even with all that canine contact, Troi seems somewhat bemused by Cami's poking behavior.

Does it mean:

1. Cami wants to play?

2. Cami wants Troi to move over?

3. Cami thinks Troi is a small, tasty snack food?

It's really hard to say.

Even though Troi ignores and doesn't seem bothered by nose pokes, to be on the safe side, we never let Cami and Troi stay alone in the same part of the house when we're not around. Option number 3 is just not something I want to deal with.

Happy Tabby

Understanding Your Cat

Once you have a cat, you are exposed to a different world. Cats perceive the world far differently than humans do. Many people who end up having "problems" with their cat, often simply haven't learned how to communicate in a way the cat understands.

In this section I'll attempt to offer a few reasons why your cat does the things she does, or at least the best guesses of experts in cat behavior. "Guesses" is the operative word, because frankly, even the experts still don't know exactly why cats behave in certain ways, or do certain things.

Cats clearly have reasons for what they do. It's obvious to the cat, but for a human, getting "inside their head" can be a challenge. The point of this section isn't so much to analyze your cat. It's to help you develop a compassionate understanding so you can try to see things from a feline perspective. Cats don't claw the furniture to "get back at you" or to be mean, they do it because it's something a feline naturally does.

Whether you're dealing with a serious and bewildering behavior problem like a cat who no longer uses the litter box, or just a cat who habitually does something a little weird, understanding why can make all the difference.

Thinking Like a Cat

Although cats aren't exactly trainable in the way dogs are, it is possible to modify their behavior. The trick is that you have to make them think that the change was their idea the whole time. So you need to think like a cat.

For example, in the feline world, food is a big motivator. If you leave food on the counters, your cat will go up there to forage, whether or not this behavior is "allowed" at your house. To counteract this counter surfing, you need a deterrent. When you are around, you can monitor her surfing. When she transgresses, you can use a squirt from a water-filled spray bottle to remind kitty that the counters are off-limits.

The most effective corrections are ones that don't involve you, however. For example, some people set up booby traps such as upside-down mousetraps underneath a piece of tinfoil. When kitty leaps up on the counter, she springs the trap, which makes a lot of noise and causes her to jump down to get away from the evil counter demon. A similar approach can be used for cats that molest garbage cans.

Cats are very territorial and have a sense of smell that is far superior to ours. They don't scratch furniture out of spite. They do it to mark territory. As most people can attest, when you yell at a cat for scratching the furniture, kitty generally just looks at you like you're an idiot and proceeds to wait until you aren't around to engage in her destruction.

A more effective approach is to keep your cat's nails trimmed and buy or make her an appealing scratching post that she can really sink her claws into. Rub the post with catnip, so she feels it's a feline-friendly place. Then attach some double-stick tape or contact paper to favorite scratching points on the sofa to make it feline-unfriendly (cats hate sticky feet). Praise the cat for scratching the post, and if she heads for the sofa, clap your hands or make another loud noise to startle her away.

The key to changing your cat's behavior is understanding what is motivating her actions. Once you understand what she's doing from a feline perspective, it's easier to find creative solutions to solve problems.

Positive Reinforcement

The term "positive reinforcement" is used a lot in training. The idea is that your cat is motivated by a reward to do whatever it is you want her to do. I tend to think of it as the "what's in it for me" approach to training. If your pet has a worthwhile reason to do something, he will do it. If you can figure out what it is that motivates your pet, positive reinforcement can be a powerful way to shape or change behavior.

Timing is the key to using positive reinforcement in training. You have to give the pet the reward at the exact instant he's doing the right thing, or the cat can associate the wrong action with the reward. For example, if you say "Fluffy, come" and the cat goes the other way, if you give her a treat anyway, she thinks she's being rewarded for stalking off. (Ooops!)

With positive reinforcement training, you only reward the good behavior, not the bad. This caveat is why so many cats continue to yowl even after being told not to. Some cats find that any attention is better than no attention. When the cat yowls, you yell. It becomes a nifty game for the cat, since you yelling is clearly (to her) part of the fun. Thus you reinforce the yowling behavior. (Another oops.)

The tricky part in using positive reinforcement as a tool is that you must find out what motivates YOUR cat. Trained cats such as the ones in TV commercials are almost invariably trained using food. The key is to figure out what type of food your cat would do just about anything for. It really depends on the cat.

Cats are individuals. Experiment to find out what motivates your pet, and keep training sessions short and happy. Once your cat figures out what's in it for him, he'll be happy to do what you want.

Friendly Kitty Behaviors

One of my cats has become the queen of "head butting." I'll be sitting on the sofa, minding my own business and she'll jump up and thump the top of her head into my stomach. It seems like a friendly gesture, but what does she actually mean by it?

Kitty head-butting and face rubbing is a form of communication. Because cats live in a very scent-oriented world, it probably doesn't come as a surprise to find out that felines have glands on their faces that secrete pheromones.

A pheromone is like a critter business card that is used to convey information to other animals of the same species. Many animals secrete pheromones of some type. These chemicals are designed to elicit some type of reaction. For example, some insects use pheromones to attract a mate.

Cats have several pheromones that they use to mark their territory and indicate their reproductive status. The pheromones secreted by the facial glands often are used to mark familiar or comfortable spaces. (Apparently, my lap is one of those places.)

When your cat rubs his face on your leg, he is essentially saying that he thinks you're special enough to rate some of his pheromones. Given the disdain that most cats have for many humans, you should feel privileged to earn this level of love and respect. Sure, he may also be demanding his dinner, but he's doing it in a very friendly way.

Inter-Kitty Communication

When you have more than one cat, you often wonder at the seemingly bizarre communication methods they have with one another. Two cats can be contentedly curled up snoring happily next to each other and then 30 seconds later, feline war has broken out. What happened?

Cats have many ways of communicating with each other, much of which we can't easily understand because our noses aren't as sensitive as theirs. As I mentioned, scent is one of the most important ways a cat learns and interacts with his environment. Cats also see very differently than humans do, so they pick up on nuances of body language we often don't notice.

Some cat owners who did not get their cats neutered soon enough may know that cats mark territory by spraying urine. In the wild, they'd be doing it on trees for all their feline buddies to smell. (In your house, you get to smell it instead, which is unpleasant to say the least, so get your cat neutered.)

Fortunately, cats have other ways of depositing their scent and marking their space. As I said, when a cat rubs his face on a table leg, scratching post, or you he's actually depositing facial pheromones. These scents mark the space and help the cat navigate through it.

Cats that like each other will rub their cheeks on each other. When they rub each other's faces, it is a sign of companionship. The shared scents apparently create a sense of harmony and well being. Basically, in the feline world, "if you smell like me, you must be okay." You may also have noticed that cats that know each other well will sniff each other's rears. This activity is actually a sign of acceptance.

Cats exhibit other body language as well. A cat with his ears forward and eyes half closed is relaxed. When he wakes up, his eyes open wide and his whiskers stand out. When your cat is scared of something, he flattens his ears back on his head and his pupils dilate. If he's angry or upset, he'll flatten his ears, push his whiskers forward, open his mouth, and make growling or hissing noises. And as all the Halloween pictures depict, a cat arches his back and puffs up to look larger when he's defending himself.

As with dogs, staring is considered a form of intimidation in the feline world. So if you see two cats in a "stare down" match, they are probably getting ready to pounce on one another. If you have a cat that's somewhat afraid of you, don't stare directly at him. Slowly blink your eyes. Looking like a sleepy cat makes you seem less scary.

Unlike a dog, a cat that is wagging her tail is not happy. She's in conflict, probably annoyed, and trying to figure out what to do next. A relaxed cat lowers her tail, and a happy, proud cat holds her tail high above her back.

Grumpy Cat Sounds

Many years ago when we got our younger cat Troi, we spent weeks listening to the older cat Alia growl as they slowly got acquainted. If you've never heard a cat growl, it's somewhat different than a dog. It's often sort of a low grrrrr, rather than a full growl. I can report that over time, it becomes truly tiresome to hear.

Recently, my sister brought her two cats with her when she came to visit. They lived in the guest bedroom separate from my two cats and the dogs. About two days after the guest cats arrived, apparently Alia noticed and started growling. She was growling at Troi, which made me wonder a) is Alia taking out her annoyance about the other cats on Troi? b) is Alia dumber than I thought and thinks Troi *is* the other cats or something?

Most people realize that growling isn't good, but in the hierarchy of feline noises, things like hissing or spitting are generally worse. In the feline world, growling is a warning that means, "look out, I'm annoyed." In this case, the cause of all the growling over the weekend was actually probably because of "non-recognition aggression."

If you have more than one cat, you may have experienced the odd situation that occurs when you bring one cat home from the vet and the second cat acts like she has never seen her feline housemate before. One theory is that the cat coming home smells different. That would also explain Alia's growling. The house smelled like "other cat" so Alia figured it must be Troi. (Okay, she was wrong, but she's also not a rocket scientist by any stretch of the imagination.)

Depending on the personalities of the cats involved, non-recognition aggression can be a serious problem. The cats may fight and hurt each other. Plus, if the cat returning home from the vet is still groggy from anesthesia, she's at a disadvantage and could be seriously injured.

If you hear growling or other aggressive behavior, err on the side of caution. Keep the two cats separate behind closed doors, so they can't get to each other. Ideally, you should put the aggressive cat in a separate room with a litter box and other necessities until he settles down. This process could take hours, so you may want to plan on leaving him there overnight.

When you go to reintroduce the cats, do it carefully as if they really were meeting each other for the first time. And realize that the problem will probably happen again, so plan on keeping the felines separate for a while after any trips to the vet or other journeys to lands that are foreign to your felines.

The Wonderful World of Kitty Whiskers

If you've ever spent time just watching your cat, you may have noticed how often your cat moves her whiskers. You might have wondered, what exactly is all that whisker wiggling about? What do whiskers do for a cat?

A cat's whiskers or vibrissae are located in horizontal rows on either side of a cat's face above his mouth. Other groups of whiskers are located above the eyes, on the cheeks, and the back of the front legs. As you've probably noticed, whiskers are much thicker than regular hair. They are attached to a tremendous number of nerves, and can move backwards and forwards.

Whiskers are sensitive to air current vibrations and help a cat navigate his world. The only thing mildly similar in humans is our fingertips. For example, when you go out sailing, you might have licked your finger and held it up in the air to determine which way the wind was blowing. In somewhat the same way, a cat can go into a dark room and tell what is in the room based on the air currents hitting his whiskers. This ability not only keeps him from bumping into furniture, but also means he can pounce on a mouse with lightning speed and accuracy, even when he can't really see the mouse.

Your cat also uses his whiskers to determine if he can fit through an opening. The whiskers are roughly the same width of the cat, so he can put his head in a small area and determine if the rest will follow. Interestingly, if your cat gets overly chubby, he loses this ability, since the whisker length is determined by genetics, not by how fat the cat is.

In addition to being useful to the cat, whiskers can also be useful to you. A cat that has his whiskers pulled back against his face, is feeling angry or defensive. If he's stalking or aggressive, the whiskers will be forward and tense. A cat with relaxed whiskers facing forward and down is happy and content.

It probably also comes as no surprise that most cats don't like to have their whiskers touched. These delicate sensory organs are extremely sensitive and if you touch them, the cat will blink. And it should go without saying that you should never cut a cat's whiskers. They aren't hair, and cutting them is just plain cruel.

The next time you see your cat wander by, watch those wiggling whiskers and marvel at how much information they give your cat every second of every day. Whiskers aren't just cute; they are a vital part of your cat's sensory perception.

Cats Don't Always Land on Their Feet

Our cat Troi, a.k.a. the Fat Cat, a.k.a. the Blob Cat, a.k.a. the Tubby Tabby, is not exactly light on her feet. When she jumps down off a windowsill, pretty much the whole house knows about it. She also is walking proof that cats don't always land on their feet.

When we first got her, she liked to sit on the railing that surrounds our stairwell. Unfortunately, one time she leaped to jump up there, missed, and went down the stairwell. She did not land on her feet. In fact, she landed on her side and when we rushed down the stairs to see what happened, I was afraid she was dead. Fortunately, she was just bruised and still has a few lives left.

Even though the old wives' tale about cats always landing on their feet obviously isn't true, because of their coordination and certain aspects of their physiology, cats often can pull off incredible landings.

When a cat falls, he actually can tell which way is up and will rotate his head up and bring his front legs up toward his face. Then the rest of his body sort of rolls upright following the front half. (If you've ever seen film footage of this process in slow motion, it's really fascinating.)

A cat's ability to right itself in midair is because of a small organ in the cat's inner ear called the vestibular apparatus. Cats also have tremendous flexibility, as you have probably noticed if you've ever watched your cat contort herself into a pretzel to clean those hard to reach areas. This ability to twist also makes it possible for them to right themselves during a fall.

Even though a cat may land on her feet, if she falls too far, the cat's legs and feet can't absorb the shock of impact and the cat may still be hurt or killed from the fall. However, you might have heard amazing stories about cats that have fallen from extremely great heights and actually lived.

Apparently, the reason for these miraculous recoveries is because if a cat falls more than five stories, it can reach "terminal velocity." When something falls, its rate of descent increases, but not indefinitely because of air resistance. Terminal velocity is when air resistance prevents further acceleration. If a cat falls far enough to stop accelerating and reach terminal velocity, the animal relaxes somewhat and spreads herself out. The impact is then spread out over a larger area and results in fewer injuries.

In any case, as any vet will tell you, cats are hurt and die in falls all the time. So keep screens on your windows and keep your kitty safe.

TROI

When Cats Thud

As I sit here typing away, loud thumping noises are coming from upstairs. Even the Gold Dog, who was sleeping heavily, looked up to make sure it wasn't a marauder or the UPS man. Nope, it's the cats stomping each other.

The Little Cat (Troi) is angry and she's taking it out on the Bad Cat (Alia). Apparently, the Bad Cat is putting up a halfway decent fight.

Unfortunately, it's my fault the Little Cat is angry. As part of the never-ending quest to keep the feline element on the day shift, I woke up the cats at lunchtime today. They were snoring profusely on a chair in the dining room. The two humans and four dogs had been upstairs enjoying lunch for a while. Generally, our presence wakes the cats up enough so that when I move the chair, they leap off, sit around and yawn for a while. Waking them up during the day makes it less likely they'll spend all night keeping us awake.

Today, as it turns out, the Little Cat was really, really asleep. As is my custom, I pulled out the chair to wake up and remove the snoozing felines. Except today, I really dumped them. The Little Cat was SO asleep, she literally rolled end over end off the chair like a log and landed on the floor with an unceremonious THUD.

After a few of those tense moments where you fret that the cat is okay, we realized she was fine. Then we burst into laughter. The Little Cat was not pleased and sat there looking seriously annoyed.

Cats don't always land on their feet. When they don't, they become very surly.

Life with Your Cat

It's odd that people send their kids to school for years, yet seem surprised when a new pet doesn't psychically know everything about living life in your house. Sadly, cats aren't omniscient, so you need to take the time to educate Fluffy about living in your household.

This section has information on taking care of your cat, giving her enough exercise, simple techniques for cleaning up accidents, and how to make sure your cat is properly cared for when you are out of town.

Playing with Your Cat

Anyone who has ever lived with a cat knows that they like to be entertained. Many cats like to amuse themselves at 3 a.m. If you value your sleep or your cat has decided that you are a great hunting target, you may want to spend some time rescheduling and redirecting your kitty's predatory behavior.

Cats require a lot of sleep. So if you play with your cat during the day, she will be less likely to keep you awake at night. (She's got to get all that sleeping in sometime!)

Cat toys don't have to be expensive. Anything that seems even remotely animated is fair game to a cat. You can tie a piece of crumpled up paper or an old sock to a shoelace and drag it so it leaps and jumps across the floor.

When you get packages in the mail, rip off any loose tape and throw the box on the floor. It's almost guaranteed that your cat will emerge from wherever she's hiding to investigate that box.

Paper grocery bags are another big hit with the feline set. After your cat gets inside, scratch the bottom of the bag and watch her flail about in there. You can even use the beam of light from a flashlight as a toy. Cats love to chase the light across the floor.

One toy to avoid, however, is you. Never wave your fingers or hands in front of your cat in a playful manner. If your cat considers your hands a plaything, she may get into the habit of scratching or biting you.

Another source of kitty amusement can be another cat. Although keeping up with two kittens or cats can be rough on the local human at first, two cats can keep each other company. Whether you know it or not, they'll probably be roaring around your house, chasing each other with tremendous feline zeal while you're away at work.

Playing with your cat can be a great stress reliever for you and great exercise for your cat. If you've been feeling harried or your corpulent cat is starting to resemble a fire hydrant, find some time to play.

Alternative Cat Toys

Cats are easily amused. Almost anything can act as a cat toy, even trash. As noted, boxes and paper bags are cat toys pretty much anyone can afford. My cat Alia, for example, gets very demanding whenever she sees us open a box.

The arrival of a UPS package can be the source of great feline excitement. Alia cares little for the contents of the box; she won't rest until we've thrown the cardboard container on the floor for her to investigate. She feels it's her job to inspect every box that comes into her territory.

Paper shopping bags are almost as good. There's a tense moment when Alia must determine whether or not she can fit into the bag. After that, the bag takes on a life of its own as she stuffs herself inside or chases it all over the house.

Although cat toys can be inexpensive or even free if you have a garbage-lover like Alia, you should check to make sure they are safe before letting your kitty have access to them. Watch out for potentially dangerous items that attract your cat's attention.

For example, Alia adores eating plastic packing tape. Obviously, plastic isn't good for her, so before she gets to play with a new box, we have to strip it of all feline-unfriendly, loose pieces of tape. Much to her dismay, some boxes are so laden with tape that Alia doesn't get to spend any time with them at all. (And we usually receive a quite surly yowl when we take them away.)

Keep an eye out for commercial toys that could be dangerous too. Thinking about how your cat plays can go a long way toward avoiding accidents. Some cats are content to just bat around toys with their paws, but if your cat likes to attempt to consume everything she comes in contact with, make sure you remove any dangling parts, strings, or bells from her toys. By taking a few precautions, you can make sure your cat can entertain and enjoy herself safely.

Cleaning Up Accidents

"Accidents" are a fact of life for pet owners. So is cleaning them up. However, the way you clean up the mess can have an effect on whether or not the animal uses that place for its "bathroom" again. Cats have a vastly more sensitive sense of smell than you do. Even though you may think a spot is clean, your cat still knows that's where he left his "scent." If you don't completely clean the area, your retraining efforts will have no effect. As long as your cat can smell his scent, he will return to the same spot.

The first step is to find all the soiled area. This involves using your nose and eyes. You may have to get up close and personal with your carpet to find old stains. You also can use a black light bulb to reveal old urine stains. Turn out all the lights in the room and use the black light to identify problem areas.

Next you must clean the areas so the odors are really gone. Remember, even if you can't smell traces of urine, your cat can. If the accident has just happened, soak up as much of the urine/liquid as possible with a folded towel or a stack of paper towels. Stand or press on this pad until the area is barely damp.

Now get an enzymatic cleaner such as Nature's Miracle and follow the instructions on the bottle. These cleaners actually neutralize the odor, as opposed to just covering them up. Avoid using cleaning chemicals such as ammonia or vinegar, since they don't eliminate the odor. Using other strong chemicals may also decrease the effectiveness of the enzymatic cleaner. Avoid using steam cleaners to remove urine because the heat can permanently set the stain.

After you have used the enzymatic cleaner, rinse the area with cool water. Remove the water by blotting again with a towel. By following these steps, you can begin the retraining process free of smells that distract your pet from doing the right thing.

Walking the Cat

When our cats were about two years old, we had to take them on a 1,200-mile road trip to move to Idaho. We knew that they'd be in strange places like hotel rooms and probably would not appreciate these unfamiliar environments. Because cats tend to run from things they don't like, we invested in harnesses and leashes, so we could hang on to them.

The idea of walking a cat on a leash may seem silly to some people, but if you have an indoor cat, taking her for a walk can be a great way to let your cat experience the outdoors safely. Cats really can be taught to walk on a leash; it's all in how you introduce the cat to the idea.

First you need to acclimate the cat to the harness. We left the harnesses out for a while, so they became part of the kitty household universe. Then we would put harnesses on the cats for short periods of time. Naturally, since it wasn't the cat's idea, initially each cat was extremely offended. However, over time, they got used to wearing their stylish new gear.

After the cats had adjusted to the harnesses, we attached a leash they could drag around. They thought it was weird, but again, they got used to it. Finally, once they were okay with the equipment, we took them out on a small adventure.

When we embarked on the move, the car with the cat carrier was packed to the gills with stuff. Because we had acclimated the cats to the harnesses, we could take them out of their carrier and into the hotel rooms attached to their leashes.

Because we had planned ahead, the cats didn't mind being leashed, and I felt a lot better. With all the stress of moving, the last thing I needed was to lose a cat somewhere in the middle of Nevada.

Taking Care of Kitty

As you go to make travel plans, don't forget about your feline friend. Someone needs to take care of her while you're gone. Although some cats have no problem staying at a boarding kennel, other cats find it so stressful that they refuse to eat. Our cats fall into the second category, so when we travel, our neighbor "cat sits" for us. That way, the feline team doesn't have to leave their familiar surroundings.

Taking care of the cats is not really very complicated. Mostly our neighbor makes sure the kitties have food, water, and that the litter box is okay. Our cats even get lots of attention and play time. Of course, not everyone has a neighbor as nice or as conscientious as ours.

In that case, you may want to hire a professional pet sitter. But finding a good pet sitter can be a challenge, especially if you're new to an area. If you are planning a trip, start looking for a sitter in advance because, like boarding kennels, good pet sitters can get booked up far ahead of time. Ask your veterinarian and any pet owning friends for a referral. Most pet sitters also put their business cards in pet stores and vet clinics, so stop by any pet-oriented places and ask.

You also can try the Internet, since a couple of the big pet-sitting organizations have Web sites. Contact Pet Sitters International (www.petsit.com) and the National Association of Professional Pet Sitters (www.petsitters.org) to get the names of members located near you.

Once you have a few names, you should interview your potential pet sitter. After all, you want the person who cares for your cat to meet (and hopefully like) your feline friend, since they'll be spending time together. A professional pet sitter should be businesslike. During the interview, most have a form they fill out with your answers to questions such as where the food and supplies are located and contact information for your veterinarian.

Professional pet sitters also generally provide written information that details their services and the costs. In addition to caring for your cat, some pet sitters offer extra services such as collecting your mail or watering your plants. Ask for a list of references and call them.

Most pet sitters will tell you that getting too little information from the client is far worse than getting too much. Be sure to tell the pet sitter anything unusual about your cat's health or behavior. For example, does Fluffy love being scratched on her tummy, but only until she wiggles her front paw just so? These little details are important. Plus, don't forget to stock up on cat food and litter before your trip. Many pet sitters charge extra for running out to the store to pick up all the things you forgot.

When you leave town, it's easier to enjoy your vacation when you know your cat is being cared for by someone you trust. Whether you opt for a friend, neighbor, or pet sitter, finding someone to care for your cat should be an important part of your vacation planning.

TROI

The Feline Dimension

Today I was talking about cats with a friend of mine. She suggested that cats sort of live in their own little world. As I looked down and saw my fat cat Troi staring off into space, I had to agree.

Cats seem to live in their own dimension: the Feline Dimension. That cat sitting there staring is living in a world we just don't understand. In the Feline Dimension sight and sound are all very well, but smells are more important. If you've ever had a cat sniff disdainfully while trying to settle into your lap, you know what I mean. It's as if they're saying, "Oh my, I can't possibly sit THERE." (Even though the cat sat there yesterday, the day before, and pretty much every day of her life.)

I think that cats only have an interest in humans at the points where the Feline Dimension intersects with ours. For example, in the Feline Dimension, O-Dark Thirty is the time of awakeness. If you're a cat, you can see pretty well in the dark, so if you want to raise a ruckus, O-Dark Thirty is the time to do it because you can annoy the most people.

Feeding time is another time when the Feline Dimension intersects with the human one. At the appointed hour (i.e., the hour appointed by the feline) it's time to start demanding food from the human element. Possible ways to suitably motivate the human may include yowling, slapping food bowls around, or splashing in the water dish.

After all, the Feline Dimension is a wondrous land whose boundaries are not of the imagination, but the cat.

Dealing with Behavior Problems

One of the ways animals and humans are alike is that they're not perfect. Even the sweetest cat can make mistakes or behave badly. When this happens, you have a responsibility to try to understand the cause of the behavior. Understanding behavior can be tough, since you can't have a heart-to-heart talk with Fluffy so she can explain why she is suddenly using the carpet as her personal litter box.

To further complicate matters, with some adopted cats, the unacceptable behaviors might be deeply ingrained from past experiences. They might even be the reason the cat ended up in a shelter in the first place. This section includes information on some common (and not so common) feline behavior issues, along with tips that should help you understand what might be causing the problem.

Think About the Pets

Life is full of changes and if you don't think your cat notices, well, you're wrong. Many times behavior problems in pets can be traced to changes in their home life. After all, they live there too. Major life events such as death, separation, or divorce cause a great deal of emotional distress and all of your pets pick up on it and become anxious. If people suddenly start shouting and arguing with one another, it has an effect on every creature in the house.

When it comes to your cat, your household and the people and pets in it are a big part of his universe. Fighting, yelling, or people or animals entering or leaving the household can disturb the cat, which can result in behavior problems.

Remember that the cat doesn't understand what's going on in the human world and you can't explain it to him, so realize that your personal problems can be a source of feline behavior problems. According to behaviorists, when a couple separates, it's a good idea for the children and the pets to stay together. Trying to share a cat between two households rarely works well, since cats are very attached to their routine. Continually interrupting and changing their daily life can lead to problems, especially with older pets.

Adding a new person into the household may cause problems for cats, especially if that person arrives with his or her own pets. It can take quite a while for everyone to adjust to the new arrangements and you should be on the lookout for problems. At first make sure to feed the animals separately and don't leave prized toys on the floor that could be the source of an altercation. Pets also may be jealous of human attention. If a cat hisses, don't correct them. Instead, simply ignore the animal and walk away. The sound of a human voice could encourage more aggression, so teach the pets quickly that any display of aggression will just cause you to walk away and not "play" that game anymore.

The only thing you can be sure of in life is change. If you have animals, take the time to try and understand their reactions when life's changes happen.

Keep Kitty Where She's Supposed to Be

People have differing levels of comfort about the placement of kitty feet. Some people believe that a cat's feet should never touch any surface where a human eats. Those surfaces include such places as the kitchen counter, dining room table, and breakfast nook.

Other people cook with Fluffy staring them in the face and don't mind when the feline residents prance through the dining room and leap up on the table during dinner. It's all in your perspective.

I fall somewhere in between the two extremes. I know where kitty feet have been (i.e., the litter box) and I really don't want those stinky paws wandering around me when I'm cooking or eating. So our cats are never allowed on the counters or tables when we are around. What they do on their own time is anyone's guess. (Although based on deductive reasoning and trace evidence, I'm thinking nocturnal counter wanderings are mighty common.)

Cats are drawn to places that have food on them because of the food. If the cats in your house have ever found food on the counters, they will never forget and they will check for more at every opportunity. If you clean up after yourself, you are less likely to have felines wandering around looking for a snack. Finding some kind of cleaner that doesn't smell good to a cat (such as citrus, for example) is even better. You may be able to keep cats away just by wiping down the counter.

If you don't want felines foraging while you are around, you need to discourage that behavior and encourage other, better behavior. For one thing, cats like to be up high. To a cat, counters and the table are high. If you give them a place off the floor that's all their own, the cats will enjoy perching there. For example, we have a three-level kitty tree. It's out of dog range and next to a freestanding cabinet. A cat who is really ambitious can leap from the top of the tree to the top of the cabinet. There she can happily be queen of all she surveys way up high.

To discourage the counter-surfing behavior, we also have small squirt bottles around the house that we use to squirt any cat that violates the "no counter" rule in our presence. Cats hate being squirted, so they don't get caught at it very often.

Ideally, behaviorists say it's better to use deterrents that work without your involvement, so the cat doesn't associate the punishment with you. For example, some people buy electronic "Scat Mats" that give the cat a tiny static shock when they land on it. The cat leaps off the mat and doesn't associate the punishment with you. A lot of other homemade booby traps are possible too. For example, we have cans filled with pennies on top of our stereo speakers. When the cat tries to claw a speaker, the can falls and scares her off.

Realistically, I can deal with having cats that know I'm not pleased when they jump on the counter. They might think less of me as a human, but they seem happy. And I don't have kitty feet near my food.

Teach Your Cat Not to Claw You

The dead mouse on the floor this morning is a testament to my normally lethargic cats' hunting prowess. Even the most domesticated and social indoor cat has the same hunting instincts that cats have in the wild. And if you're not careful, you can inadvertently teach your cat to direct its hunting attention toward you.

Most people who have trouble with feline aggression in their household "played rough" with their cats when they were kittens. It may be cute when a kitten plays with your feet; it's a lot less cute when the 12-pound cat attacks you every time you come in the room.

When you play with a kitten, be sure to direct its play toward a toy. By always displacing the attention to the toy, you'll probably never have a problem with kitty aggression in the first place. If the problem already exists in an adult cat, take the same approach. Anytime the cat goes for you, try to distract it with a favorite toy. If the cat still prefers attacking you when you offer the toy, squirt the cat with a squirt bottle or plant mister filled with water. Say "no" at the same time you squirt to reinforce the fact that you disapprove of the behavior.

Skip to the Loo

Many cats end up at animal shelters because of "loo problems." In other words, something has gone wrong with the use, misuse, or lack of use of the litter box. Often the cat has taken issue with some aspect of the litter box and refuses to use it.

When you get a cat, one of the first questions you will be faced with is where to put the litter box. It needs to be easily accessible. Hiding it in the farthest corner of the basement or garage that is freezing in winter is going to make your cat less inclined to visit. The box should be close enough to the rest of the house that the cat will make the journey, but far enough away to keep it private. For example, we have our cats' litter box in the laundry room.

It should go without saying, but the litter box should always be accessible to the cat. If you have dogs, you want to make sure the box is also not accessible to them. Some people put the litter box into a closet and cut a cat door into it. We used a hook latch on the door to the laundry room that has a long hook that holds the door open wide enough for the cats to get through, but not the dogs. (When we humans go into the room, we just unlatch it.)

The litter itself may also be a point of distress for the cat. Many cats dislike deodorant litters or have a preference for a particular type. Some cats prefer the finer-grained scoopable litters because they are easier on the paws. Our cats prefer clay litter, since that's all they've ever known. Which brings up a point: if your cat likes the litter, don't switch.

Experts say that you should have at least the same number of litter boxes as you have cats. However, it's not always necessary. Our two cats have shared a litter box for years without incident. But some cats will block another cat from getting access, so if it seems like this situation is transpiring, invest in another box before it becomes a real problem. Put the new litter box in a different location, but that's still readily accessible.

Some cats also take issue with the box itself. If you have a covered litter box, your cat may find that the enclosed space isn't big enough for her to do what she needs to do in there. Other cats may like the more private feel. Some cats don't like plastic liners or litter that's too deep. The cat may even hate the smell of whatever you are using to clean the box. If your cat starts avoiding the litter box, consider all these possibilities and any recent changes you've made.

Speaking of cleaning, it should go without saying that cats are less likely to use a litter box that isn't cleaned regularly.

You wouldn't want to use a filthy bathroom would you? Well, neither does your cat.

When Kitty Won't Go Where He's Supposed To

Cats are normally fastidious creatures. So people are invariably surprised when kitty decides that the litter box is no longer the place to relieve herself. Unfortunately, as any veterinarian will tell you, "inappropriate elimination" is not an uncommon problem. If your cat has been happily using the litter box for years and suddenly has a problem, it could be a medical issue, so first take the cat to the vet. Only after you have determined the cat is fine, is it time to look at behavioral issues and her environment.

As a rule of thumb, any time your cat exhibits a new behavior problem, you should rule out medical reasons first. For example, when I looked up "increased urination" in a veterinary database, I found 92 possible diagnoses. Urinary tract infections are relatively common, especially in male cats, but the problems could be related to anything from kidney problems to thyroid diseases.

After your vet has ruled out any medical cause for the house soiling, it's time to look at behavioral reasons. The first is sort of obvious: the cat hates the litter box for some reason. The reason may be that the litter box is gross because you never clean it. Cats have limits, so try cleaning the box more often. Also, if you have other pets, sometimes they will terrorize the cat, so kitty doesn't want to visit the box. In that case, you need to get another box and make sure kitty can use it in peace. Otherwise, the cat may find another place that she likes better than where you have put the litter box. Once a cat has gone in a place, she'll do so again unless you clean the area really thoroughly with an enzymatic cleaner. A good rule of thumb is to have as many litter boxes as you do cats, plus one (i.e., if you have two cats, have three litter boxes). Not everyone needs to do this, but if you're having problems, it's an inexpensive experiment.

If the cat is urinating on vertical surfaces, he may be spraying, not just relieving himself. When a cat sprays, he doesn't squat; he lifts his tail and it quivers. If you see this behavior, you have a different problem. Although spraying is most prevalent with unneutered male cats, neutered males and even female cats will spray.

Marking

Cats live in a scent-oriented world that we can never completely understand. As territorial animals, they communicate, "I was here" by spraying or "marking" their territory with urine. With their superior sense of smell, a cat can tell days later who or what has traveled through his territory.

Because spraying is a marking behavior, cats are usually doing it when they think there is a threat to their territory. Perceived threats could be a new cat or other pet in the house or other change. Some cats will spray inside, even if the threatening cat is outside.

When a cat marks the local trees while out on a neighborhood constitutional, nobody really cares or notices. But when the cat starts marking the walls or the sofa, the humans in the house tend to get quite upset. Unfortunately, many people confuse this type of marking behavior with a house-soiling problem. It's not. Animals tend to mark vertical surfaces and frequently mark if they feel threatened.

Marking problems tend to happen most frequently in households where one or more animals are not spayed or neutered. Even if the cat doing the marking is neutered, the presence of an intact animal may compel the pet to mark territory.

Cats also often mark territory if they have conflicts with other animals in the home or even ones outside the home. For example, if one cat intimidates another cat, the cat being intimidated may express his anxiety by marking territory. Similarly, if the cat has conflicts with another feline he sees wandering through the yard, he may mark the house to prove it's "his."

Cats don't understand the concept of revenge, so they aren't spraying to "get back at you" for something. Sometimes they do spray out of frustration though. Think about recent life changes. Has anything happened recently that has changed your cat's world? Sometimes when the human takes a new job, for example, the cat becomes frustrated because of the lack of contact and play time.

The obvious first step to help with marking problems is to get all your pets spayed or neutered. Spaying or neutering may solve the problem completely.

Fixing the cat removes any hormonal element that could be causing the spraying problem. See if you can figure out when and where the cat is spraying and thoroughly clean the areas with an enzymatic cleaner such as Nature's Miracle. Also look into products you can spray on surfaces that deter spraying. Again, remember that cats live in a scent-based world. Just because *you* can't smell it anymore, doesn't mean the *cat* can't. Otherwise, your house can end up being one giant kitty toilet.

If the cat has been marking for a long time, you may also need to take steps to break the pattern. Try to make favorite marking spots inaccessible, or if that's impossible, change the area somehow so it no longer seems like a prime marking spot. For example, one trick is to move the feeding area to a marking spot because animals won't soil an area where they eat.

To reduce the anxiety level, you may need to find ways to resolve conflicts among the people or animals in your home. Sometimes working out issues may involve giving up an animal, having new family members work with an animal, or consulting a behaviorist.

Again, always remember that cats aren't people. They aren't marking the house to "make you angry." Working through these problems takes time, so understanding and patience on your part are required to resolve marking problems.

As with most behavior problems, look at it from your cat's point of view. If you can understand what is causing your cat to do what she's doing, you are that much closer to dealing with it.

Furniture Clawing

I have talked to many people over the years who have expressed enormous frustration with their cat's clawing behavior. Although clawing is a natural feline activity, many cats end up in shelters after destroying expensive furniture. If Fluffy is clawing your great-grandmother's antique sofa, all is not lost. There are things you can do to help encourage Fluffy to claw elsewhere.

First you need to pay attention to when and where your cat scratches. Cats have individual scratching preferences. For example, one of our cats inevitably claws when she wakes up from a nap. She does a long horizontal claw-stretch thing. So for her, the ideal scratching item is not a vertical kitty tree, but rather a horizontal board. Our other cat likes to claw vertically, so she uses the tree. (And no, neither one of them uses the sofa.)

If a cat scratches in a particular place, he is more likely to scratch there again because when a cat scratches, he releases pheromones from glands in the skin of his paws. Clawing and scratching behavior has as much to do with marking territory as it does with sharpening claws. Because scratching is a natural activity, a cat is going to claw something. It's what they do. For a house cat, your furniture is the obvious likely candidate, unless you give the cat a better alternative.

When dealing with cats, it's always best to make it appealing for the cat to choose what you want. If you don't want your cat to scratch the sofa, you need to give him something better to claw. Some cats, including ours, find sisal rope to be the ideal clawing surface. So we made a sisal rope tree and two sisal boards for them to claw.

When the cats feel the need to scratch, they go over to the board or tree and claw profusely. We usually say complimentary things, so they know that using the board or tree is a fine, fine thing. The board is an 18-inch long 1x10 piece of scrap pine wrapped with sisal rope. The total cost was about $2.50 at the most, so anyone can afford it. Our kitty tree is a three-level "tripod" tree that we made out of scrap plywood and a 5-inch diameter branch that fell down during a storm. It too was really cheap to assemble; it cost maybe $10. We wrapped the center pole of the tree with sisal rope and covered the platforms with old carpet. The second level has a hole cut in it so the cat can run up the pole, and through the hole to the second level.

Of course, the cat may want to test a number of new clawing frontiers, so after redirection, the next step is to discourage your cat if he claws some place you don't want. We use squirt bottles and say "no" to indicate to the cat that clawing other places is a bad plan. When our cats were kittens, as soon as we saw them claw anything "bad," even a little bit, we'd pick them up and hold them up next to the sisal rope-covered pole of the kitty tree until they reached out their paws. They'd instinctively reach for the tree and latch on. Since they were small, they had no choice but to scurry up. This proved to be a great way to teach them that the tree was theirs and it was a lot of fun to claw.

In addition to kitty furniture, you may also want to think about your furniture as well. When you are shopping, think about the sofa from your cat's point of view. Some sofas are made of cloth that just looks like it was made to be clawed, and collects hair like a magnet. Generally smoother fabrics are better; sometimes, just a less appealing slipcover can make a big difference. If your cat has already decided your sofa is a scratching post, you can try putting strips of double-stick tape on the claw spots to discourage further activity.

Finally, it may seem obvious, but keep your cat's claws trimmed. A cat with huge claws almost can't help clawing everything by just moving around the house. It also should go without saying that long claws can do a lot more damage than short ones.

Of course, sometimes all your plans don't work and the cat insists on scratching something you care about. In that case, talk to your vet. A nail-covering product called Soft Paws is available and of course declawing. However, declawing really should be used as a last resort and never should be done on cats that go outside. It's major surgery, so talk to your vet about the potential long- and short-term side effects.

ALIA

Zoomer Kitties

Anyone who owns cats would know that we have felines in residence the moment that they walk into our house. Many signs are evident as soon as you enter the living room, most notably the garbage on the floor. As noted, what other people may deem trash, our cats consider playthings. So at least one scrunched and thrashed paper bag or box is almost always lying on the floor somewhere.

Other big clues are the cans sitting on the speakers. A few years ago, one cat decided that speakers make great scratching posts. As I mentioned earlier, we put some pennies in a can and balanced it on the edge of the speaker. If the kitty touches it, the can falls off and scares the bee-boops out of the cat. The can is a free, recycled, insto-deterrant.

The bad news is that loud music also causes enough vibration to make the cans fall off. I discover this problem periodically when I jump up and down on my mini-trampoline. About 50% of the time, I forget to remove the cans before I start playing music at high volume (sometimes I gotta blow the dust outta the Bose). So there's a rude shock when the can falls off.

The cats really get into the whole music scene. Loud music makes them weird. (Okay, maybe it just wakes them up.) But while I am exercising, they often zoom around the room chasing each other. It's quite entertaining to watch the felines rock out. Between the falling cans and the zoomer kitties, there's just a whole lot of action. Who says exercise is boring?

Grazing Kitties

A few years ago, our neighbors asked us to take care of their houseplants. They spend the winter someplace a lot warmer than Idaho, and they didn't want to drive their three huge spider plants halfway across the country. So we agreed to tend to the plants over the winter. Spider plants make great hanging plants and we already had hooks in our ceiling, so the plants could hang in front of our picture windows.

Unfortunately, we also have cats. By the time we gave the plants back the following spring, the plants had no little "spiders" or leaves hanging off the side that was closest to the window. One of our cats apparently spent most of the winter launching off the windowsill and dive-bombing the plant. Needless to say, our neighbors have never had us plant-sit again.

Plant eating is actually a normal feline behavior. Cats eat grass and other plants because it's good for their digestion. And of course because they like eating plants. Given that cats are the ultimate hedonists, you're going to have a lot of trouble convincing a cat not to eat your plants. You'll be fighting feline instinct and desire, which is not a good thing.

As with most kitty-behavior issues, diversion is probably your best bet. You can buy seeds for grasses cats like to eat at many pet stores. Or if you don't want to get an official seed "kit," try planting some wheat grass or catnip in a tray or flowerpot, so your cat can have her own private snack bar. The idea is that if the cat has her own little garden to munch on, she'll avoid your other houseplants.

If diversion doesn't work, you can also try deterrents. Pet stores sell non-toxic, bad-tasting concoctions that you can spray on the leaves of your plants. However, you should read the label carefully as some sprays can hurt the plant.

Keeping your cat entertained (not to mention tired) also can keep her from chowing down on your plants. A sleeping cat is not committing acts of kitty badness. So play with your cat and make sure she's got a scratching post and fun toys to keep her amused.

Finally, when you buy houseplants, be sure that they are not poisonous to cats. If your cat is an inveterate plant eater, she may not be particularly discriminating. A few common plants like philodendrons and poinsettias are toxic. Your vet may be able to give you a list of plants to avoid, or you can find a list online at the Humane Society Web site at http://www.hsus.org/pets/pet_care/protect_your_pet_from_common_household_dangers/common_poisonous_plants.html.

Chatty Kitty

Most cats make some kind of noise. For example, I have one cat that squeaks. Rather than mustering for a full meow, she makes little squeaky noises. My other cat, in contrast, yowls mighty yowls instead of meowing. A little meowing here and there doesn't bother most people, but what do you do if you have a cat that just won't shut up?

First you should figure out why your cat is making noise. Sometimes cats meow if they aren't feeling well. If your normally quiet cat is anxiously vocalizing, it may be because of a medical problem. Since cats often don't exhibit any signs of illness until something is seriously wrong, you should take her to a vet as soon as possible.

Cats also often may begin making noise if there is some kind of transition in their lives or they are grieving about a perceived loss. And some cats such as Siamese cats are just plain vocal. Many cats aren't any particular breed, but if your cat is long and lean with a pointy face, odds are there was a Siamese somewhere in her background. Vocal cats like these often meow to get attention.

In any case, assuming your cat doesn't need veterinary attention and you don't want your cat to be a constant source of racket, the best approach is to ignore the cat when she vocalizes. Although ignoring the cat can be difficult, many cats "talk" because they know you will react. Remember that to many animals, even a bad reaction is better than no reaction. Even if you yell at her, lock her in another room or outside, or make loud noises, in her mind, the cat still has gotten what she wanted: your attention.

To discourage an attention-seeking cat the only solution is to act as if the cat isn't there. Then when she is quiet, give her lots of attention, treats, or playtime. By encouraging the behavior you do want, over time you can extinguish the behavior you don't want.

I Am Cat

I am cat

Hear me snore

In sunlight

Too bright to ignore

When it's cold and gray during the winter with no sunlight anywhere, our cats worship the God of Warmth (i.e., our pellet stove). For those who don't know, a pellet stove looks sort of like a wood stove, but it burns pellets made out of pressed sawdust instead of logs. Unlike a wood stove, it can be controlled by a thermostat; the stove calls for heat and draws pellets in from a big hopper.

In any case, during the long days of winter the cats get into the habit of loitering around and staring at the pellet stove, whether or not it is actually on. Alia, the elder feline, loves to stare into the flame. I think that, like pretty much everyone else in the house, she gets tired of the cold. It's a bummer to be a heat-worshipping cat in deepest Idaho.

Keeping Your Cat Healthy

Keeping your adopted cat healthy is a lot like keeping yourself healthy. It all starts with regular hygiene, grooming, exercise, and tooth care, plus regular checkups at the doctor's office and preventative medicine like vaccinations.

It also means administering medication when your cat is ill, and maybe even researching all your options, like nutritional supplements or holistic medicine. Even the most healthy, low-maintenance, ultra-fit feline needs an annual health check and basic preventative medicine. If you've chosen an older cat as a companion, you'll need to be extra vigilant about her health.

All cats should be protected against the health problems caused by fleas, ticks, and other external "nasties!" But first, let's start with the source of all critter health, no matter what the age or background of your cat: good grooming.

Grooming

Imagine how you'd feel if you never brushed your hair. Cats have a lot more hair than you do, so no matter what the breed, every cat requires some sort of regular grooming.

Over time, cats that are never groomed can develop mats that pull on the skin and cause extremely painful irritation. You may have seen Persian or other longhaired cats that have had to be shaved because the mats got so bad. This kind of neglect is lamentable not only because of the effect it has on the animal, but because grooming can be an extremely enjoyable experience for both your cat and you.

Brushing Your Cat

When you get a kitten, you should introduce her to the grooming process as early as possible. Even though your kitten may just have "baby fur," getting her used to the process can be helpful later in life when her full coat grows in.

Make grooming a happy process, but start small. Like all youngsters, kittens have an extremely short attention span, so begin by stroking her gently and quietly handling her paws, ears, and mouth area. Over time you want to work up to being able to touch all her pads and toenails, look in her ears, and open her mouth and touch her teeth. Praise the kitten when she stays calm and quiet. If she loses interest, don't push it. Give her a toy and go play with her somewhere else.

You want your cat to always associate grooming with something good. After the kitten is used to being touched and handled, introduce the brush. Speak to her in a soothing voice and tell her how wonderful she is as you brush her back. For many animals, the feel of a brush tugging her fur may be a new sensation, so go slowly.

You can use the same technique with adult cats as well. It may take a little time if a cat has not had much experience being brushed before, but with lots of patience and praise, the grooming process can be fun for everyone involved.

Trimming Your Cat's Claws

If you've never trimmed your cat's claws, the prospect can be daunting. I know it's not exactly one of my favorite things. But it must be done. You can use a couple of types of trimming tools. Some people use plain old human nail trimmers, but I find them difficult to use (and hold the cat at the same time). The most common type of kitty toenail trimmer looks like a pair of very short miniature scissors.

When you trim claws, a lot depends on the cat. One of my cats is extremely cooperative because I've been trimming her claws since she was 8 weeks old. I pick up the cat and cradle her in my arms. I grab a front paw, and start trimming. My other cat, Troi, is less thrilled with the idea, so I often have to hold her by the nape of the neck to convince her that we are doing "the claw-trimming thing" even though it was not her idea. (Troi is fundamentally opposed to almost anything that is not her idea.)

If you have an uncooperative cat, find a friend to help you hold the cat while you trim. If your cat is really seriously against the idea, it can help to wrap her in a towel. Another option is to purchase a "cat bag" which is basically a zippered bag that confines the cat's body, so just the head is sticking out. You can partially unzip the bag and remove a single paw at a time without worrying about what the other three paws might do to you.

When you trim the nail, clip off only the end. Cats have nerve endings and blood vessels inside their nails called a quick. If your cat has light colored nails, the quick looks like a dark line. You do not want to accidentally trim so close that you hit the quick. It can be difficult to see the quick on cats with dark nails. So be very careful and trim off just a little bit at a time.

If you accidentally clip too much, the quick will bleed. If this happens, apply pressure to the tip of the nail or dab on some styptic power. When it's over, give the cat a treat or pet her and tell her how wonderful she is. With any luck, next time will be easier.

Washing Your Cat

To many people the idea of washing a cat is ludicrous. After all, most normal healthy cats keep themselves quite clean all by themselves. However, a number of situations can warrant kitty bath time. For example, if your cat gets into something disgusting, whether it's oily, smelly, or sticky, you will want to clean it off, rather than let your cat throw it up all over your house.

Bathing the cat also can help allergy problems. Interestingly, many people who are allergic to cats aren't allergic to the fur, but cat saliva. If this is the case, just soaking the cat with water (i.e., without using soap) can be enough to reduce the allergic reaction. Of course, when warmer weather arrives, you also may need to give your favorite feline a flea bath.

No matter what the reason, giving a cat a bath doesn't have to be a traumatic experience. The first thing to do is trim the cat's toenails. (The reason for this should be obvious.) If your cat has long hair, next you should groom her. Contact with water will tighten any mats in the fur, so you should remove them before bath time. As a side note, if you have a new kitten, getting her used to being washed when she's still a kitten is a very good idea.

When you are ready for the event, get all your gear in place. Place a rubber mat or towel at the bottom of the sink or tub, so your cat has a good clawing surface (that's not your leg). Depending on your cat's preference, you may want to have water already in the sink or tub as well (to reduce the potential trauma of the sound of running water). If you have one, a hand sprayer attachment makes it much easier to soak the cat. Also be sure to use shampoo specially designed for cats. Using other shampoos for dogs or humans can be dangerous because cats can absorb chemicals, which may be poisonous, through their skin.

When you wash, be prepared for kitty unhappiness. Yowling, crying, and carrying on is par for the course. If you have trained your cat well and she knows not to scratch or bite humans, it will be a reasonably painless process.

If you have a cat that does not go along with the washing program willingly, you can try putting the cat into a lingerie bag. (For those who don't know, a lingerie bag is one of those mesh bags people use to wash their "delicates;" most 'five and dime'-type stores sell them for about $2.) When the cat is in the bag, the water and soap go through, but claws do not (or fewer of them anyway). The idea is that you can douse and lather up the cat without Fluffy attempting to rip all the skin off your arms.

When you are done, be sure to dry the cat thoroughly with a towel (this is the fun part for the cat) and let the cat snooze away the afternoon in the sun. Cats have short memories, so she'll forgive you for your transgression...eventually.

Dealing with Fleas

When cold weather starts to arrive, you may get a few unpleasant houseguests: fleas. Just because "flea season" is supposed to be over does not necessarily mean that the fleas go away. Often, they just move inside. Of course, in some warm areas, every season is flea season.

If you have outdoor cats, fleas may be hitching a ride inside your home, so they can enjoy a more comfortable environment. Fleas can reportedly jump as high as 13 feet, so it's easy for a flea to jump on a dog or cat and come inside.

With that in mind, you should check your pets regularly for signs of fleas.

When you check for fleas, look at the warmest parts of your cat, such as the underside where the back legs meet the body. Even if you don't find an actual flea, you may find evidence, such as eggs or "flea dirt." Fleas live off the blood of your pet and flea dirt is the partially digested blood they excrete.

It's easy to tell flea dirt from regular dirt. Just put some on a flat surface and add a drop of water. If the dirt turns red, you know it's flea dirt. Another thing you may or may not find is flea eggs, which are white and about the size of a grain of sand.

If you find evidence of fleas on your cat, the fleas are in your house as well. Fleas start laying eggs within the first 48 hours of their first meal. They can lay 40 to 50 eggs per day, and a female flea can produce more than 2,000 eggs during her lifetime. Even though not every flea survives, this tremendous ability to reproduce means that you never have "just a couple fleas."

To deal with a flea problem, you absolutely must treat every pet in your household. You need to treat the pets, the house, and the yard at the same time. If you don't, the fleas just relocate.

In the last few years, many advances have been made in flea treatments. Products exist that make it possible for you to successfully treat your pets, house, and yard safely and effectively. To find out which products would work best for your cat and your environment, consult your veterinarian for specific product recommendations and options.

TROI

Toenail Time

I've noticed that my creativity comes in bursts. I've discovered that whether writing or designing, I need to ruminate first. It may look like I'm just sitting and staring, but really I'm festering with big thoughts.

Unfortunately, Troi, the small tank-like feline doesn't get this process at all. She sits and glares at me for a while. Then she stretches a paw up to my chair to reach out and touch my thigh. Unfortunately, it's claw-trimming time, so this ostensibly friendly gesture causes some degree of pain. (And doesn't do much for the creative process either.)

The Troi-cat is the epitome of self-absorption. She lives by the philosophy that anything that is not her idea is not a good thing. She's actually an affectionate little critter, but only on her terms. If it's not her idea, she's not interested. For example, taking pills is SO VERY not her idea. Ever.

However, I have slowly convinced her that at our house, we do the regular claw-trimming thing whether she likes it or not. It's getting better, but she's still somewhat obnoxious about it. Part of the problem is that I got her as a 5-month-old teenager, instead of as an ultra cute 8-week-old kitten. Teen ogre-hood had already set in and there was no turning back.

Anyway, clearly it's time to have another special claw-trimming moment with the small cat. She's sleeping peacefully now, but the big evil toenail trimmer approacheth.

Health Care

A healthy cat is always easier to live with than an unhealthy cat. Many behavior problems are related to chronic pain, intestinal parasites or disease, chemical or nutritional imbalances, or neurological problems. If your adopted cat was undernourished, injured, or experienced severe physical trauma like exposure to extreme cold, you might need to pay extra attention to her health and work closely with your vet.

In this section, you learn about some common (and not so common) feline health issues, and what to do if your favorite kitty gets sick.

Nine Lives

If you love your cat, you probably want her to get the most out of her nine lives. You can do a number of things to help your cat live a long and healthy life.

1. Keep the cat inside. Statistically, indoor cats live to be an average of 13 years old (although some indoor cats may live beyond the age of 20). Conversely, the average life span of an outdoor cat is less than three years. You may think that your outside "barn cat" is coping with the great outdoors, but there are many hazards that contribute to the shorter life span of outdoor cats. Wild animals, diseases, cars, poisons, and getting lost are just a few of the rigors indoor cats don't have to deal with.

2. Spay or neuter. At around 6 months old, get the cat spayed or neutered. Getting a cat "fixed" eliminates a number of health problems, many behavior problems, and the possibility that your cat will contribute to the pet overpopulation crisis.

3. Feed her well (but not too much). Be sure to give your cat plenty of food and water. But don't overfeed her, as overweight cats are susceptible to various health problems, especially as they get older.

4. Vaccinate. Keep your cat current on all her vaccinations. Whether you take her to a veterinarian or give the shots yourself (assuming you know how), the vaccinations can save your cat's life.

5. Get to a vet. If your cat starts acting differently for some reason, something may be wrong with her. You know your cat better than anyone, so if you suspect a problem, take her to the veterinarian. Many illnesses and problems can be treated if they are caught early.

Few things are as comforting as a purring cat in your lap. Return the favor and be good to your cat. With a little effort on your part, you can keep your feline friend healthy and happy for years to come.

Choosing a Vet

When you get a cat, one of the first things you need to do is find a veterinarian. If you've adopted a kitten, you need a vet to give all those important vaccinations and also to get your furry friend off on the right paw medically. Even if you've adopted an adult cat, you should take her to the veterinarian for a checkup at least once a year.

The next obvious question is how do you find a veterinarian if you've just moved to a new town or you've never had a pet before? Of course, first you can check the local yellow pages to see who is out there. Many listings give you an address so you can determine if the vet clinic is near your house. It's not just a convenience issue; your proximity to the vet clinic can make a difference if you have a veterinary emergency.

You also can look online for vet clinics. Various vet locator sites exist and many veterinarians have their own Web sites these days, so you can learn a little about their facility from the convenience of your keyboard. If you adopted your cat from an animal shelter, they may also provide a list of local veterinarians. (Often they are prohibited from actually recommending a specific clinic, however.)

The best way to find a veterinarian is to just ask around. Odds are good that someone you know has animals, so they'll undoubtedly have opinions on veterinarians. (When we moved here, one of our cats was sick, so we got a recommendation from the realtor who sold us our house.)

After you've made a selection, you may want to go to the clinic without your critter first to talk to the vet and check out the facility. Many vets will let you set up an "informational" appointment like this so they can get to know you. This visit is your chance to check out the clinic. Is it clean? What do you think of the staff? Are the other animals there totally freaked out or just (naturally) nervous? How does the vet seem to treat the other patients and staff?

Of course, you may find that your neighbors were wrong and you don't like the vet they recommended. Just because someone else says they love a particular veterinarian doesn't mean that vet is right for you. Veterinarians are people and sometimes people get along and sometimes they don't. If you feel intimidated or uncomfortable in any way, you probably should keep looking.

When you establish a good relationship with your veterinarian, you should be partners with a common goal:

your pet's health. So you always want to understand what your vet is telling you. Ask questions and keep asking until you understand the medical advice he or she is giving you. Vets see your cat for only a few minutes, so they rely heavily on information from the owner to diagnose problems. Your cat can't say what hurts, so your observations are important. If you can't communicate well with the vet, your pet is the one who loses.

Taking the time to find a veterinarian you like and who will care for your cat is time well spent. Assuming your cat lives a long healthy life, you may get to know your veterinarian very well.

The Feline Physical

Many people avoid going to the doctor, except when they are sick. But even if you won't take yourself in for a physical, you should take your cat in for a veterinary exam at least once a year. Unlike a human, a cat can't tell you when he's not feeling well. Cats are often incredibly stoic about pain, so you may not realize there is a problem until it is quite advanced. As with people, early detection is key to treating many illnesses. Plus, cats have a much shorter life span than humans and a lot can change in just one year.

The bottom line is that making that effort to get your cat in for her annual physical is the single most important thing you can do to maintain her health, so don't put it off. Many veterinarians also give vaccinations during the annual exam. But other than shots, what exactly is the vet doing when he peers and pokes around Fluffy?

Vets have special training to detect subtle changes that may indicate illness. Generally, during the exam, the veterinarian will listen to the cat's heart and lungs, look in the mouth, eyes, and ears, and palpate the body to look for any unusual lumps or bumps.

At the same time, the veterinarian will ask you about any changes you've observed in your cat's behavior. Don't be afraid to bring up even small things. You see your pets every day, and it's easy to overlook small differences over time unless you pay attention. If there have been any changes in eating habits, weight gain or loss, vomiting, coughing, sneezing, or behavioral changes, be sure to report them to your veterinarian. Even if something seems a little "odd," or your cat is acting "funny" in any way, tell your vet.

Depending on your cat's health history, the veterinarian may also suggest "blood work" to screen for certain diseases and organ functions. Yearly blood screens can help your vet spot various problems before they become serious. The vet may also recommend a fecal exam to check for worms or other parasites.

As your cat ages, your vet may suggest more frequent exams. Since every year of a dog or cat's life is equivalent to between 5 and 10 human years, pets over the age of 6 or so may develop age-related problems that can progress quickly. Just as a 40-year-old human shouldn't wait 10 years to have a physical, a 6-year-old cat may need to go to the vet's office more than once a year.

You and your vet are on the same team: you both want to see your cat live the longest, healthiest life possible. Getting your cat in for her physical exam is the best way to prevent or treat potentially devastating diseases. The best medicine is always preventative medicine. At the exam, the vet can diagnose and treat problems early, so you can enjoy life with your furry friend as long as possible.

Cat Vaccines

Vaccinating your kitten or cat is an important part of responsible pet ownership. It's an inexpensive way to protect your feline friend from a number of serious diseases.

Generally, vaccines are given as an injection (read: a shot). Often the vaccine will be a "combination" that protects against several different diseases. Outdoor cats are often vaccinated against rabies and the feline leukemia virus.

Vaccinations are particularly important for kittens. Generally, it's a series of "kitten shots," that are given at periodic intervals to provide the best immunity. You should discuss the specific vaccination schedule for your cat or kitten with your vet, but here is some information about the vaccines and the diseases they protect against:

Feline panleukopenia is sometimes called feline distemper, although it isn't related to canine distemper. This viral infection is actually caused by the feline parvovirus, which is similar to the canine parvovirus. Like canine parvovirus, feline panleukopenia attacks the gastrointestinal tract causing fever, vomiting, and diarrhea. Feline panleukopenia used to be a leading cause of death in cats, although it is much less common now thanks to effective vaccines. Young kittens are particularly susceptible to the virus and the prognosis for kittens under the age of 8 weeks is not good.

Feline viral rhinotracheitis (FVR) and feline calcivirus cause 90% of upper respiratory infections in cats. These extremely contagious respiratory diseases can lead to death from pneumonia in kittens. Sneezing, runny nose and eyes, and coughing are the primary symptoms of an upper respiratory infection. Although the viruses are very contagious, cats must be exposed to an infected cat or come in contact with toys or people who have been around an infected cat to become ill, so it's more common in environments that have cats living in close proximity to one another.

Feline infectious peritonitis (FIP) is a fatal disease caused by a coronavirus infection. The virus is a relatively uncommon disease, but the incidence is much higher in areas where large groups of cats are housed. Kittens, older cats, and cats in poor health or experiencing stress are most susceptible. Although a vaccine exists, studies have not yet confirmed how effective it is.

Feline Leukemia (FeLV) is a retrovirus that causes immunosuppression in cats. Before administering a feline leukemia vaccine, usually a cat or kitten is tested first to make sure the cat is not harboring the virus. Outdoor cats are at risk of contracting FeLV, and although there is no known cure, it's easy to prevent by vaccinating the cat.

Rabies is a viral disease that causes brain swelling in mammals. Vaccinating a cat against rabies protects you (and other people) as well as the cat, since rabies can be transmitted to humans. Outdoor cats should be vaccinated; the laws regarding the frequency vary, so check what the rules are in your community.

Opinions differ as to how often booster shots should be administered to cats. Cats can develop a cancer called feline vaccine-associated sarcoma near the spot the shot was given. Because of this risk, some vets are recommending a longer interval in between booster shots in older cats. However, all kittens and young cats should "get their shots." The risks of the diseases far outweigh any other concerns, so be sure to talk to your vet about shots when you get a cat.

The Declaw Debate

Declawing, i.e., removing the claws from a cat is a hotly contested issue in the humane community. Some behaviorists believe declawing is psychologically harmful to cats because scratching is a natural feline behavior. Other people feel that if the choice comes down to dumping the cat at a shelter (or something worse) versus getting it declawed, surgery is a better option.

Cats scratch for a number of reasons. They will claw something to remove the outer sheath of their claws, to stretch, and to mark territory. Cats actually have scent glands in their paws, so the reason they claw the same place over and over again is because they can smell the scent on the surface.

Note that even if you declaw a cat, a number of the reasons for clawing remain, so kitty will still go through the motions of scratching. Obviously, the cat can't do as much damage to the sofa, however.

Declawing a cat is not minor surgery. Although there are two main techniques, both involve removing the end of the toe. While the cat is under anesthesia, the preferred method is for the veterinarian to use a scalpel to cut open each toe, carefully remove the last bone segment, and close the wound. Because the cat must be anesthetized, many people have the surgery done at the same time the cat is spayed or neutered. It's important to give your cat some time to recuperate and it's vital that the cat be an inside-only cat from then on.

As more people have become educated on options to declawing, the surgery is performed less often. Some veterinarians won't do it at all. The cats here at my house are inside cats that have all their claws. I taught my cats to use their scratching post or "kitty tree." My mother still can't quite believe I was able to do this, but it was easy.

We have a tall sisal rope kitty tree. When the cats were kittens, we'd carefully "hang" them on the tree, which forced them to climb up, since cats can't go backwards down a tree. As soon as you hold them close, the kittens automatically reach out and attach themselves with their claws and off they go. All the kittens we've done this with thought the trick was a whole lot of fun, so the tree became their favorite clawing location and sisal their favorite clawing surface.

As any cat owner will attest, the key to training a cat is to make the cat think the trick was her idea.

Post-Surgical Pet Care

After you bring your cat home from spay, neuter, or other type of surgery, you need to give your furry friend a little extra TLC. Often the veterinarian will give you post-surgical advice, but in the excitement of bringing Fluffy home, it's easy to forget what they told you.

When you bring your cat home, she may be a bit sleepy or groggy from the anesthetic. Some types of anesthetic may make your cat drool or seem more uncoordinated than usual. Anesthetic also can cause nausea, so the evening after surgery, you should give the cat access to water, but avoid feeding.

As caretaker, your job is to keep your cat as comfortable and quiet as possible so she can heal. If you have kids or other pets, keep them from bothering the patient for at least 24 hours. For three to five days, it's best to keep the patient indoors because you want to keep the cat away from excessive hot, cold, or wet weather. In other words, right after surgery, you really shouldn't just let the cat out to roam the neighborhood.

While your cat is healing, be sure she avoids strenuous exercise or play. You should check the incision area twice a day and look for any bleeding, excessive swelling, redness, odor, or drainage. Some minor swelling and redness may occur, but contact your vet if you see a wide gap or tissue protruding from the incision.

It's also important to keep your cat from licking or chewing at the incision, no matter how much she may want to fuss at it. This type of excessive attention can result in torn stitches, slow healing, or infection. (If the cat is successful in ripping out the stitches, you may need to bring her in for another surgery!) Some critters absolutely won't stop licking, so you may have to either buy or borrow an "Elizabethan collar" or E-collar.

A number of types of E-collars are available, but the traditional type is essentially a plastic cone that fits over your cat's head. Pretty much every animal that has ever worn one hates it. The annoyed patient may bang into walls, furniture, doors, the floor, and you. She may give you dirty looks and appear completely morose. Don't feel guilty! It's important that you don't take off the E-collar, unless you can keep an eagle eye on your cat. You really don't want to have to go back to the vet for an infection or incision repair.

Depending on the surgery, your cat may or may not need to have stitches removed. If there are stitches, they generally need to remain in place for a week to ten days. After a week, the incision should be sealed. If there is no discharge, pain or redness, your cat is probably just about healed.

Assuming you've done your monitoring job well and you get the okay from your veterinarian, your post-surgical caretaker duties are over and you and your cat can go back to your normal routine.

Dental Care

Most people don't think about their cat's dental health, but it's important. Although cats don't often get cavities, the plaque and tartar on their teeth can cause gingivitis and periodontal disease. Without treatment the teeth can decay and eventually fall out. Veterinarians see many a toothless cat whose owners ignored dental care.

Healthy teeth aren't just a cosmetic nicety. Another less obvious side effect comes from the bacteria that cause the decay. These bacteria can actually travel through the bloodstream and damage major organs. Cats with bad teeth can become very sick.

When it comes to dental care, prevention is important. Just as you go to the dentist regularly (we hope), you should take your cat in for regular dental checkups at the veterinarian. Almost any time you take your cat into the vet, you've probably noticed the vet checks the cat's mouth. He's looking for yellowy crusty tartar and plaque on the teeth and red along the gum line that indicates gingivitis.

If your vet finds problems, he or she will let you know that it's time for a cleaning. Called a dental, prophy, or prophylaxis, this procedure is a thorough cleaning and polishing of your cat's teeth. The cat must be anesthetized for the procedure, although many vets do let the cat go home the same day.

Afterward, the veterinarian may recommend home tooth brushing. I confess that personally even though I floss my own teeth every night, brushing my cats' teeth just isn't going to happen. I accept my limitations and realize that it means I have to take the feline team in for teeth cleanings more frequently than if I regularly brushed their teeth myself.

If brushing the cat's teeth isn't working out, your vet may recommend specially formulated foods that help reduce the accumulation of plaque and tartar. Various treats also may help. Generally, cats who eat dry food are less susceptible to periodontal disease than those that eat wet food. Some breeds of cat may also be more likely to have tooth problems because of the shape of their head.

If you take your cat in for yearly exams, don't be surprised if your vet recommends dental care. It's just another aspect of basic "kitty maintenance."

Ear Mites

When was the last time you looked in your cat's ears? Last week? Last year? If you haven't looked in there lately, you probably should. Cats are generally very fastidious about their upkeep, but there are certain problems that even the tidiest cat can't deal with.

If your cat scratches her ears or shakes her head a lot, it may be a sign that she has ear mites. When you look in your cat's ears, they should be free of any debris. If you see a reddish brown or black buildup of waxy stuff in the ear canal or detect any kind of nasty smell, your cat probably has some kind of infection or ear mites.

If you suspect any kind of problem, do not try and treat it with home remedies. Ear mites, although common, can develop into a serious condition that if left untreated can potentially kill your cat. Take your cat to your favorite veterinarian for an examination.

A number of simple and effective treatments exist that can cure ear mites quickly and safely. Although treatments vary, your veterinarian will probably thoroughly clean the cat's ears and treat them with a topical medication to kill the parasites. He or she also may advise you to continue to treat the cat at home for a while. Ear mites are contagious, so if you discover that one of your cats has ear mites, you should treat the other cats in your household at the same time.

Ear mites can be a difficult parasite to get rid of, and like fleas, you really don't want them on your cat or in your house. It's not an invasion of feline privacy to check your cat's ears, so do it regularly. Your cat will be glad you did.

Hairballs

Most cat owners are familiar with the "hack, hack" noise of their favorite feline hurling up one of those lovely wads of cat hair known as a hairball. Because cats groom themselves by licking their fur with their raspy tongues, hair is collected on the tongue and then swallowed.

If enough hair goes into the kitty's stomach without passing into the intestinal tract, the hair has to go out the way it came in. That's when you hear the lovely noises as your cat attempts to vomit. Some cats are more disposed to hairballs than others and it doesn't necessarily have to do with the length of their hair. Although longhaired cats are likely to get hairballs, shorthaired cats can get them too. I have two shorthaired cats that look almost exactly alike. One hacks up hairballs frequently; the other has never had a hairball in the seven years we've had her.

If your cat gets hairballs frequently, it's easy to treat the problem. You can buy "hairball remedy" from your vet, pet supply store, or catalog. These preparations basically coat the stomach and combine with the hair so it will pass through the intestine and then out. Because hairball treatments are flavored, most cats like the taste and will eat them willingly. If not, you can smear some on the cat's mouth and paws so she'll lick it off.

Hairballs are a common problem that is easy to cure, but be alert for other problems. If your cat seems lethargic, has stopped eating, or if the vomiting continues for more than two or three days, the problem may not be hairballs, so call your veterinarian as soon as possible.

Feline Diabetes

Recently, my mother found out that her cat has diabetes. Zeus, the large orange tabby, has always been what one could politely call an "enthusiastic" eater. As a result, he's one hefty feline. Diabetes is most likely to strike older, obese male cats, so Zeus is not unusual.

There are two varieties of diabetes. Type 1 is caused when the pancreas fails to produce enough insulin. In humans, this type is often referred to as "juvenile diabetes." Type 2 diabetes is caused by an inadequate response of the body's cells to insulin. This type is the one that often occurs later in life and can be related to being overweight.

The good news for my Mom and Zeus is that with some extra care, diabetic cats can generally live out their normal life span and remain happy and healthy. Unlike humans, cats don't suffer from diabetic complications, such as vision or circulatory problems.

The signs of diabetes are similar to some other much worse feline diseases, so for some cat owners, a diagnosis of diabetes may come as a relief. Diabetic cats often will drink a lot of water and urinate more. Sometimes they also lose weight.

Although there is no cure for diabetes, it can be managed with medication and diet. In many cases, the veterinarian will recommend insulin shots to manage the disease. As I told my mother, giving a cat a shot is really not such a bad thing. (In fact, if you ask me, it's a lot easier than giving a cat a pill!) The needles are very small. If the cat is relaxed and so are you, the process can be quick and virtually painless. I read about one owner of a diabetic cat who gives the cat a treat after every shot. As soon as the cat hears her take out the needles, he comes running over.

Most cats require shots one or two times per day. Every cat responds differently to insulin, so it takes some time working with your vet to get the dosage right. If the cat is obese, the vet will also put him on a gradual weight loss program. Because managing diabetes requires such close communication with your veterinarian, be sure you have a vet that you feel comfortable talking to and working with.

Although the diagnosis may be upsetting and you may be afraid of needles, your cat can live for many years with diabetes if you make the commitment to care for her. Even with diabetes, your cat can give you love and companionship for years to come.

Toxoplasmosis

Cats are sometimes dropped off at animal shelters because the owner is pregnant. These people often are not very well informed and know just that there is "some disease that pregnant women can get from cats," so they get rid of the cat. However, even though the disease is dangerous to the unborn baby, a few common sense precautions can prevent transmission.

The disease is called toxoplasmosis, which is caused by a protozoan called Toxoplasma gondii that a cat can pass in its feces, and it is dangerous to the child the pregnant woman is carrying. A cat can get the protozoan if it eats an infected bird or rodent, so indoor cats rarely are affected. If a human handles the cat's feces by cleaning a litter box or gardening in soil where a cat has eliminated and then ingests the feces or soil, he or she may become infected by the parasite. If the person is a pregnant woman, this infection can then be passed to the fetus and cause serious neurological damage to the baby.

If you are pregnant, be sure to talk to your doctor and your veterinarian about toxoplasmosis. Your (human) doctor can run a blood test for toxoplasmosis to determine if you have antibodies that would make you immune to the disease. If you discover that you are at risk, ideally you should have someone else take over litter box duty for 9 months and avoid working in soil unless you are wearing gloves. If no one else is available to take over the litter box chore, just wear rubber gloves while cleaning the litter box and afterwards wash your hands thoroughly.

Every pregnant woman must take special care of herself and avoid risks during her pregnancy for any number of reasons. But you don't have to choose between your baby and your cat. If you want to continue to have the companionship of your favorite feline during your pregnancy and afterward, just take a couple more precautions and everyone will be happy.

Upper Respiratory Infections

Just like people get colds, cats can get viral infections that make them sneeze, snuffle, and get watery eyes. And much in the same way a cold can run through a child's kindergarten class, cats can get the feline equivalent by associating with other cats. Outdoor cats or cats exposed to other felines in shelters or boarding kennels may get what's referred to as an Upper Respiratory Infection (URI).

A URI refers to an infection that is centered around the sinuses, eyes, nose, and throat. Two viruses are responsible for most upper respiratory infections: herpesvirus-1 and feline calcivirus. A bacterial infection called feline chlamydia is also responsible for some feline URI cases.

The bottom line is that if your cat starts sneezing or has a nasal discharge or watery eyes, she may have an infection. Although the infection itself generally isn't serious, complications can arise, especially in young kittens. These youngsters often don't have a fully developed immune system and may develop fatal cases of pneumonia or other serious problems.

Because the infection is often viral, there may not be a lot you can do. However, veterinarians may prescribe antibiotics to help prevent secondary bacterial infections. They may also prescribe drugs to alleviate some of the symptoms or to treat complications such as eye ulcers.

As with a human cold, the best way to prevent URIs is not to get them in the first place. Vaccinations exist that can prevent the diseases. Keeping your cat healthy with good food and a healthy lifestyle will bolster her immune system, so she'll be more resistant to viruses.

If you work or volunteer at places that have sick cats, be sure to wash your hands frequently. When I used to work at vet clinics and shelters, I would remove my shoes, change all my clothes, and wash my hands before getting near any of my animals. (The "contaminated" clothes and shoes were put away where prying snouts couldn't sniff them.)

You also should take precautions when introducing a new pet to your household. If you foster cats or adopt new ones, be sure to isolate the new arrival for a while to ensure you don't infect your existing cats.

Think about where you adopt your pets as well. Sanitation and isolation procedures have been well known and in place at many shelters and humane societies for years. They fight a daily battle against incoming disease, yet still some places don't take the necessary precautions to prevent disease.

So with that in mind, if you see a shelter full of sick cats, you should be ready for your cat to get sick, even if he doesn't exhibit any symptoms when you adopt him. Feline URIs can take a while before symptoms appear. The odds are good the URI will break out at some point after you get your feline friend home. Just be ready, take him to the vet, and give him the care he needs.

Kitty Weight Loss

When I moved to Idaho, one of the first people I met was a veterinarian. At some point during the awful packing event that preceded the 1,200-mile road trip to North Idaho, one of my cats stopped eating. We didn't know when Chani, the smaller and more neurotic of our two gray tabbies, stopped relishing her food, but we noticed when she started vomiting evil green slime instead of eating.

If your cat loses weight, it should be cause for concern. In a 10-pound cat, a 1-pound loss represents about 10% of her body weight, which is significant. Although a small weight loss may just be a part of a cat getting older or a finicky nature, it could be a symptom of a serious problem such as kidney failure, hyperthyroidism, feline leukemia (FeLV), feline immunodeficiency virus (FIV), or cancer.

Needless to say, after we got to Sandpoint, we hustled Chani to the vet. Her weight loss wasn't due to any kind of disease as it turned out. The vet couldn't find anything obviously wrong with her, but cautioned us that some cats stop eating due to stress. If we couldn't get her to eat, Chani's liver could fail and she'd effectively kill herself. We tried tempting her with cat food and feeding her extra B vitamins to stimulate her appetite.

Another possibility was that Chani might have eaten something like packing tape (there was a lot around) that was obstructing her digestive system. After a day or so of her still not eating, we took Chani back to the vet for a "barium series." She was fed barium, which is a mildly radioactive substance that shows up well on x-rays. Her x-rays showed nothing unusual in her system.

However, after the yummy barium and staying overnight at the vet clinic, Chani came home hungry. No one knows why barium cured my cat, but apparently, it's not unusual. So, the moral of the story is if your cat loses weight, take her to the veterinarian.

Pilling the Cat

At some point in your cat owning career, the veterinarian will probably innocently tell you that you need to give your cat a pill. You may not think it's a big deal until you get home and then wonder how exactly you are going to get that large pill into that small uncooperative feline.

The easiest way to give a cat a pill is to put it in food. If you are lucky enough to have a cat that wolfs down anything put in the food bowl, he may not notice the pill. Of course, this approach only works if your cat eats all his food at one sitting. If the cat doesn't eat it all, she might either miss the pill or not get all the medication.

Some cats may tolerate a pill hidden in a special treat like a bit of tuna, cheese, or canned cat food. Sadly, my cats tend to know I'm up to something, so this approach never works for me, but some people report success if they give the cat some of the food first minus the pill, then sneak the pill into a later treat.

If food doesn't work, you have to take the direct approach. You might have seen your vet quickly open the cat's mouth and stuff in a pill. Years of practice make vets good at the process; I can assure you, it's not as easy as it looks.

First take a moment to get yourself ready. Make sure the pill is out of the bottle and very nearby. Getting the pill into the cat is a two-handed process. Basically, you use one hand to open the cat's mouth and the other to place the pill as far back in the cat's mouth as you can.

The trick to opening the cat's mouth is to have your hand over the cat's head and grasp one side of the jaw with your thumb and the other side with your fingers. You press in a bit on the hinge of the jaw, and tilt the cat's head back. The lower jaw should open, so you can use your other hand to put the pill in as far back as you can get it.

When the pill is in, close the cat's mouth and hold it closed. You can try stroking her throat or blowing gently in her nose to stimulate her to swallow. Unfortunately, many cats are good at spitting out pills, so you may have to go for a second try.

Plus, once you've gone through the process once, the cat is wise to you and will be less tolerant of later attempts. It can be helpful to wrap the cat in a towel to keep her in position. Of course, having someone to help you hold the cat is even better. Here's another hint: If you have to pill your cat, you might want to check the claws first. If they are really long, a nail trim is a good idea. Think about doing the trim long before you plan to give the pill. Most cats get annoyed being "messed with" too much in one sitting.

It is helpful to have your veterinarian show you the pilling process before you leave the clinic. Some vets also sell a special "cat piller" device that can help with difficult felines. If it's really a problem, you should ask about possible alternatives to pills.

Caring for Your Older Cat

Like all of us, our cat Alia is getting older. She is 12 years old and getting to be a senior kitty. Although "geriatric" status for cats is said to be around 13 years old, Alia is definitely looking like an older cat. Her once full and beautiful tail has gotten skinny and her muscles aren't as toned as they used to be. But she can still zoom around the room and put the obnoxious younger cat in her place when necessary.

Most indoor cats live to be 12 to18 years old. Outdoor cats normally only live to be 4 or 5 years old because they are more likely to be hit by a car or subject to other accidents or diseases. As cats age, they sometimes develop health problems, so it's especially important to pay attention to your cat as the years go by.

While your cat is happily snoozing in your lap, take the time to run your hands over his body and be on the alert for any potential problems. Early diagnosis is important for pets too.

You should contact your veterinarian if you notice any changes in your cat's physical appearance, behavior, or eating habits.

Like any pet, your senior cat should have access to good food, water, and clean living conditions. You also should avoid overfeeding your cat. As cats age, their metabolism slows down and they often sleep more, so it's easier for them to gain weight.

On the other end of the spectrum, if your cat is losing weight or stops eating, it can signal liver or kidney problems, so be sure to discuss any weight changes with your vet. If your cat is overweight, your veterinarian may recommend special "low cal" food. Although your senior cat may not be as agile as she once was, you should still make time to play with her because she still needs her exercise.

If your cat has particularly bad breath, it can signal illness. Tooth or gum disease is likely in older cats, so you may need to get her teeth cleaned. If the smell is more than just bad "cat breath," and seems odd in some way, it can signal diseases such diabetes, liver, or kidney disease. Excessive thirst is another symptom of diabetes, which is fairly common in older cats.

Like older people, older cats may develop vision or hearing problems. If you notice your cat bumping into things, try to avoid rearranging your house too much, so he can adapt. Deaf cats actually can be taught to respond to hand signals. Many also are sensitive to vibration, so they will still respond to some loud noises. As your cat's vision and hearing declines, it's even more important to keep her inside for her safety.

As your cat ages, you can still enjoy time with her, even if it's not in exactly the same way. You may not be able to play acrobatic "chase the mousie" type games anymore, but you can still play in a somewhat more sedate way. Older arthritic cats also often love being massaged. Kitty massage can be soothing for the human, and it's good for the cat's joints and muscles too.

Caring for an older cat isn't really very different from caring for a young cat. Just be sensitive to changes, add a little extra dash of TLC, and you'll enjoy many happy years together.

TROI

Gifts for the Stove God

As I've written, as long as you have garbage or pests, you have cat toys. Bags, boxes, and bugs are all fair game.

Given that we have animals that are not exactly particular about what they eat, I'm always really careful not to drop any packing peanuts when we receive packages. Packing peanuts are evil and nasty for any number of reasons, but the worst one is that they fly everywhere. It can be difficult to extract the artifact within the box when it's packed with peanuts without causing a polyethylene hailstorm. The static in our dry-air environment can leave you looking like some half-melted snowman.

One day, I got a package from a client. I thought I had successfully extracted all the items and took the box of evil peanuts downstairs. Unfortunately, I apparently missed one peanut.

As I sat quietly at my computer, I heard lots of rattling and clanking upstairs. This type of noise usually means one or more cats are up to no good. It turned out that Troi had found the wayward peanut and was endlessly obsessing on it.

Unfortunately, Troi loses almost every toy she has because she boots them ALL under the stove. When Troi spends hours staring at the stove, it's usually not a good thing. It means she's undoubtedly lost something under there. So we have to take out the stove drawer and figure out what lurks amidst the dust and dog hair. Getting the stove drawer out and properly back on its tracks is as frustrating as trying to figure out one of those iron blacksmith puzzles.

As it turned out, the obnoxious noises and clanking were her collar and tags hitting the floor as she reached and reached under the stove to extract the peanut. Eventually, she was successful and punted it down the stairs.

That's when I took it away and foiled her fun. But not for long. I'm sure it's only a matter of time before she finds more garbage to bat under the stove.

Keeping Your Cat Safe

Because cats are not people, they don't understand that cars are dangerous or that eating certain things can kill them. Concepts like "dangerous highway" or "toxic chemicals" just aren't part of their world. And like small children, sometimes cats are just too busy following their nose, indulging their instincts, or just plain having fun to look where they're going... and that can get them into trouble.

This section will help you protect your cat from common feline dangers that lurk in our backyards, driveways, and homes, as well as offer some special precautions you need to take during certain seasons and holidays.

Kitty Proofing

When you get a new kitten, you need to think about things from their perspective. Like little children, kittens test new items by touching and tasting them. For the safety of your new companion, you should pet proof your home. Here are a few of the things you should look out for inside and around your house:

1. Various cleaning supplies, bleach, pesticides, and fertilizer can all be toxic. Be sure to store them safely out of reach.

2. Electrical cords. Secure cords away from inquisitive kitty teeth or secure the cat away from cords.

3. Automatic garage door openers. Pets are often crushed by garage doors, so check to make sure that no animals are hiding nearby before you close the door.

4. Sweets, especially chocolate can make pets seriously ill.

5. Toys can be hazardous if they fall apart and big pieces are ingested. Carefully monitor your pet's chewing habits and take away any problematic toys.

6. Cigarette butts can cause nicotine poisoning if eaten.

A little time pet proofing the house can avoid some serious emergency trips to the vet. No one likes rushing a sick or dying cat to the emergency clinic, so kitty proofing your home is time well spent.

....

ALIA

Of Rugs and Rodents

One night, I heard a cat cavorting around our bedroom. I figured she was chasing her favorite kitty toy: a round sparkly ball. This activity can be very cute in a kittenish kind of way, but not at 2 a.m. So I got up to get the ball and hide it somewhere. The cat (Alia) ran out of our bedroom and headed down the stairs. I followed her, intent on confiscating the annoying toy. On the stairs, I found the cat and reached down to grab the ball. I discovered that it wasn't a ball, but actually a little mouse face staring up at me.

I screamed and ran upstairs. I was going to hide but instead decided to be brave and find some slippers. (No one likes rodents crawling on bare feet...eww!) I went back down armed with an empty yogurt container (with lid) to catch the mousie. Alia was non-plussed, but I did capture the rodent and placed the yogurt container in the hall closet where he could rest for the remainder of the evening. Four dogs, one cat (Troi), and one husband slept through this entire escapade, by the way.

The next morning, I noticed that both cats were staring at the closet. It turned out there was a reason for that. The rodent had apparently managed to move the container, so it fell off the shelf. The container landed on its side and the mousie chewed his way to freedom. Later, my husband James decided to deal with the situation and began pulling the junk out of the closet. He pulled out stuff and the mousie hid behind more stuff. This went on and as James got to the last box, it was clear the mousie was going to make a break for it. So, instead of pulling the box out, he threw a cat into the closet.

Troi grabbed the mouse and James took it from her, so he could relocate it. This year's mousie capture number twelve is now vacationing somewhere in the forest over on the next ridge. And I still don't like rodents.

....

Poisonous Plants

Plants are another part of your home environment that you should take into account in your kitty proofing efforts. We tend to take plants for granted, but not all of them are safe.

Certain houseplants are poisonous, including: chrysanthemum, poinsettia, pot mums, spider mums, arrowhead vine, Boston ivy, colodium, drunk cane, philodendron, neththytis, parlor ivy, amaryllis, azalea, creeping charlie, majesty, elephant ears, Jerusalem cherry, umbrella plant, ripple ivy, mistletoe, English ivy, and narcissus.

Various common outdoor plants can be poisonous to your cat as well. Here's a list of some of them:

Daffodils, skunk cabbage, foxglove, ground cherry, soap berry, rhubarb, spinach, tomato vine, buttercup, water hemlock, mushrooms, moonseed, angel's trumpet, jasmine, morning glory, periwinkle, rhododendron, lily of the valley, nightshade, and bleeding heart.

Certain trees and shrubs also can be a problem. Watch out for horse chestnut, pain tree, all types of yew, English holly, balsam pear, almond, peach, and cherry.

A complete list of poisonous plants is available online at the Humane Society of the United States Web site:

http://www.hsus.org/pets/pet_care/protect_your_pet_from_ common_household_dangers/common_poisonous_plants. html

The issue of poisoning shouldn't be taken lightly. If your cat is inclined to eat plants, be sure to remove the plant or the pet, so the animal can't get at the plant. If you suspect that your cat has eaten any type of poisonous substance, be sure to contact your veterinarian immediately!

Antifreeze

In the fall when people are busily gearing up for winter, part of the "winter preparedness program" often includes either changing or adding antifreeze to the car. Unfortunately, because of its sweet flavor, antifreeze is tempting to both pets and kids.

Antifreeze may seem innocuous because it's so common, but ethylene glycol, the active ingredient in most antifreeze and some windshield washer fluid products, is a deadly poison. According to the Humane Society, tens of thousands of animals die every year due to ethylene glycol poisoning. In fact, they assert that antifreeze is one of the most dangerous household hazards to animals and children that exists.

The reason that ethylene glycol poisoning is so common is twofold. First, dogs, cats, and kids (especially young ones) investigate new things with their mouths. Everyone knows that dogs chew, cats lick, and little kids put everything into their mouths.

Second, even though it's a fatal toxin, antifreeze made with ethylene glycol is sweet and actually tastes good. A tiny amount is extremely poisonous and fatal within hours. The signs of poisoning include excessive thirst and urination, lack of coordination, weakness, nausea, tremors, vomiting, rapid breathing, rapid heart rate, convulsions, diarrhea, and paralysis. If you suspect poisoning, you need to take your pet to the veterinarian at once to avoid an extremely swift and painful death.

You can do a number of things to keep your kids and animals safe. The first and most obvious change you can make is to put a different kind of antifreeze in your car. A number of antifreeze products are now formulated with propylene glycol instead of the deadly ethylene glycol. These newer formulations work just as well as the old fashioned version, but aren't hazardous to humans or animals (and they even taste bad).

If you do use ethylene glycol-based products, be sure to keep your pets inside while you change your antifreeze. Don't spill any on the ground and if you do, clean it up immediately. Don't dump the old antifreeze into ditches or drains. You should always dispose of used antifreeze properly at a site that takes hazardous waste.

What to Do if You Suspect Poisoning

The old saying "curiosity killed the cat" is unfortunately often true. All too frequently, cats get into poisonous substances. Cats may find medications or eat an animal that has been poisoned, such as a rodent or bird. Strychnine is the toxin used in many rodent poisons, and it affects the neurological system. People often don't think about the fact that when you put out gopher or mouse bait, you can end up unintentionally poisoning the local feline populace as well.

If you see your cat eating a poisoned animal or the bait itself, get the cat to your veterinarian as soon as possible. However, you may not always see your cat in the act of eating something she shouldn't. Pesticides used on lawns, flea treatments, cigarettes, various mushrooms, antifreeze, and many other common household products are toxic to cats.

Many over-the-counter medicines such as acetaminophen (which is used in Tylenol and various cold products) are also potentially lethal to cats. Sadly, many accidental poisonings happen when an owner attempts to medicate a cat without consulting a vet. Doing so is often fatal because cats are far more sensitive to acetaminophen than dogs. Just one tablet can actually kill a cat.

Unfortunately, poisoning can be difficult to diagnose, especially if you don't see what the cat ingested. However, if you notice your cat seeming especially sluggish or depressed, keep a particularly close eye on her. The effects of some poisons don't appear for days or even weeks. If your cat has any type of seizure, starts vomiting, loses her appetite, or has difficulty walking or breathing, call your veterinarian immediately.

At the vet's office, your cat will be examined and probably receive a number of tests in an effort to diagnose the problem. Antidotes exist for a few poisons, so if you have a suspicion as to what the poison may be, tell the vet. Of course, the best antidote to poisoning is not to let it happen in the first place. So "pet proof" all areas that have potentially dangerous substances and be sure to read product labels carefully before exposing your cat to any products, such as flea treatments.

Holiday Precautions

If you have a pet or are thinking of getting a new pet over the holidays, you should take a few special precautions for the health and safety of the critters in your house. Animals tend to find all those special holiday items fun to play with or explore. Kittens are notorious for getting into absolutely everything. Don't let your holiday turn into a tragedy. Every year veterinarians treat animals for electrocution, ingestion of foreign objects, burns, cuts from broken glass, and poisoning from toxic plants or chemicals.

So with that in mind, think about how you can pet proof the following:

Christmas Tree: Pets may knock it over, so you can either keep it in a room that can be closed off or put a barrier around it, such as baby gates or a portable kennel fence (this can help keep kids safe too). Keep those sharp pine needles swept up because they can cause intestinal problems if they're ingested.

Plants: A number of holiday plants are poisonous to pets, including holly, mistletoe, and poinsettia. Make sure they are placed where your pets can't get to them.

Ornaments/decorations: Tinsel, glass ornaments, electrical cords, and various edible decorations all can cause problems if they are ingested. Make sure they are secured so animals cannot get to them.

Food: chocolate, alcohol, and caffeine can make pets very ill, or even kill them in some cases. Do not give your pets any holiday food and keep platters of goodies out of their reach.

If you are thinking of getting a cat or kitten during the holidays, put a LOT of thought into it first. Getting an animal at any time requires a lot of thought and research. Add the normal distractions and activities of the holidays into the equation and you may put an undue amount of stress on yourself and the animal. That's often not a great way to start a relationship.

A cat is not a toy that can be returned or tossed aside when little Joey gets bored with it. Too many animals end up abused, dead, or in shelters around the holidays, so think long and hard about the temptation to get a pet during this time.

Part of the spirit of the holidays revolves around generosity and thinking of others. If you extend this feeling to your pets along with a little common sense and good judgment, everyone will have a safe and happy holiday season.

Finding a Lost Cat

At animal shelters, statistically speaking, the return-to-owner rates for cats are dismal. When I was volunteering at a shelter near my house, one year they returned 240 dogs to their owners, but only 18 cats. One reason the return rate is so low for cats is because most people wait a long time to tell the shelter they've lost the animal.

If you care about your cat, realize that any cat that goes outside MUST wear identification of some kind. You can microchip the cat or buy an inexpensive collar and ID. Many cat owners don't put collars on their cats because they think collars will be dangerous. However, the risk of losing your pet is a lot greater. Most cat collars now either stretch or break away if the cat gets caught on something. Many animal shelters give away free ID tags, so it's cheap insurance against a lost cat.

If you do lose your cat, here are a few things you can do to increase the likelihood you will find it. First, and most importantly, start looking immediately. Call all the local animal shelters as soon as you realize the cat is gone. People tend to wait days and even weeks before they call. Some animal shelters only hold stray animals for three or five days, so a cat could be lost and adopted (or euthanized) all in the same week. Dozens of cats come into shelters every week; there's no reason to think that yours wouldn't.

After calling shelters, walk around your neighborhood. Most cats don't stray very far from home. Talk to your neighbors and anyone else who walks through your neighborhood such as the letter carrier. It's astonishing how many people don't bother to ask their neighbors if they've seen a cat lately. Look in any feline-friendly hiding place such as under a porch.

Make up flyers with a picture, a description of the cat, and your contact information. Give these out to everyone and hang them on every free bulletin board you can find. It's also a good idea to make posters out of brightly colored poster board with the words LOST CAT in 2-inch letters, so people can see it as they drive by. Place the smaller flyer with descriptive text and a photo in the middle and below it put a brief description like GRAY MALE TABBY, again in 2-inch letters.

Then run an ad in the local papers. Many newspapers will run lost/found ads for free. Leave items with a familiar scent outside your home, such as the cat's litter box to help your cat use his sense of smell to find his way home. Finally, keep looking. Cats are often found weeks, months, or years later by owners who didn't stop trying.

Cat FAQ

When your cat chatters at the birds outside the window, what is she really trying to do? And why would your cat eagerly sniff something... only to make a weird, disdainful face?

In this section, I answer some of the questions we've all asked, like "why do cats purr?" and "what is the deal with catnip anyway?"

How Much Do Cats Sleep?

If you've spent any time with cats, you've probably noticed that they spend a lot of quality time snoozing. In fact, cats sleep anywhere from 13 to 16 hours per day. In other words, your friendly companion feline spends approximately 2/3 of his entire life in dreamland.

Cats sleep more than almost any other mammal. Realistically, your cat sleeps about twice as much as you do. How much an individual cat sleeps depends on his age, hunger, the temperature, and the weather. Like humans, cats go through both Rapid Eye Movement (REM) and non-REM sleep. Although no one can actually ask a cat, the assumption is that your cat dreams during REM sleep. You may notice his whiskers twitch or his eye moving behind his eyelids. The deep non-REM sleep is when the cat's body grows and repairs itself.

As with other aspects of your cat's behavior, you should pay attention to how much he sleeps. Some variation in sleep habits is normal, but if you find your cat is sleeping more or less than usual, it may indicate a problem. If you notice any change in sleep habits, you should contact your veterinarian.

A cat that seems lethargic or depressed may be ill. Conversely a cat that is sleeping less than usual may have a thyroid problem. Although dogs are more often hypothyroid (meaning they don't have enough thyroid hormone), cats are more likely to be hyperthyroid (meaning they have too much thyroid hormone). Because the cat is producing extra thyroid hormone, his metabolism goes up, and he sleeps less.

Most cats, particularly house cats, do a lot of their sleeping at night. People who have cats that wake them up in the middle of the night often say their cat is "nocturnal" although that's not technically true. Cats are "crepuscular," which means they are most active at dawn and dusk. They do their hunting at these times because their prey is most active. During the heat of the day, the cat is asleep. Although they have good night vision, they can't see in the dark, so they tend to sleep then as well.

If you have a cat that wakes you up early every morning, she may simply be reacting to her crepuscular nature. When the sun comes up, the cat wakes up. At certain times of year, dawn is undoubtedly going to happen before your alarm clock goes off. (It helps to have very thick curtains in your bedroom to keep the light from waking up you or your cat.)

Of course, you also can inadvertently reward your cat for getting you up too early. If you feed her in the morning, don't feed her right after you get up. Don't ever respond to feline demands either, or you are doomed to be awakened by your cat forever.

Finally, if your cat has turned around her schedule, so she is on "the night shift" wake her up during the day and play with her. After all, the animal needs 16 hours of sleep, so it's got to happen sometime.

ALIA

Switching to the Day Shift

A long day is made even longer when you haven't gotten enough sleep.

We can thank the feline crew for this sleep interruption because apparently they are now on the night shift. "Sleep all day, romp all night" is their new motto. I'm here to tell them that things are about to change. Romping is noisy business, and when the first thing I hear in the morning is a feline yowl, it puts me in a foul humor.

The bad news is that if you don't pay attention, cats will become nocturnal. Realistically, they need 16 hours of sleep, so naturally they have to sleep during the day to log that many zzz's. But I've found that if I make an effort to wake them up during the day, they won't wake ME up at night.

Of course the "wake up the cats" program is not met with great joy from the wake-ees. Sometimes I can get canine assistance. When we all come upstairs at lunchtime, the canines like to see what the felines have been up to, so much snuffling ensues. (It's really hard to sleep when you're being snuffled, apparently.)

In any case, today's great awakening project seems to have been successful. Even now the cats are sitting on the stairs glaring at me about the current lack of food.

But they are awake. Which means I should be getting a good night's sleep tonight.

Why Do Cats Purr?

The question of why cats purr sounds like a simple one, but there is a fair amount of dispute on the topic. As most people know, domestic cats purr when they are contented. A purring cat is generally a happy cat. And if you have spent a lot of time with a happy cat in your lap, you have probably noticed that the cat purrs both when she inhales and when she exhales. (I have one cat that gets so happy she purr-snorts.) Often two cats will purr while grooming each other to indicate happiness and contentedness.

Because kittens are born blind and deaf, one theory as to why cats purr is that the mother cat's purring is a physical sensation that the kittens can feel to help them find Mom so they can nurse. The kittens begin to purr in response when they are less than a week old. The theory here is that the kittens purr to tell momma cat that they are getting their milk and everything is going okay. Although cats can't meow with their mouths closed, a kitten or cat can purr with her mouth closed, so the kitten can purr and nurse at the same time.

Not all purrs are happy purrs, however. Deep purrs may indicate that your kitty is in pain. Some cats purr when they are injured or dying. Other cats purr when they are afraid or distressed. Sometimes cats also purr when they are anticipating something good, such as food (one of my cats purrs whenever she sees me with the food container).

Because it's very difficult for the "experts" to examine the innards of a cat while she's purring, no one seems to really know exactly why or how cats purr. It seems that purring is sort of a Zen thing. Cats purr because they can.

What's with the Weird Face?

It's easy for cats to look offended. We can tell when there's something disgusting on the floor because our cat Troi will sniff, look up at us with a weird look and her mouth half open. We refer to this display as the "open-mouth sniff," and it means she's found something really gross, so we generally go investigate and clean it up. As it turns out, she's not just making faces. Troi has a real reason for opening her mouth when she smells something.

A cat's sense of smell is fourteen times that of a human. In addition to being able to smell with their nose, cats also have a special sensory organ called the vomeronasal organ or Jacobson's organ. Located in the roof of the cat's mouth behind the teeth, the Jacobson's organ consists of two fluid-filled sacs that connect to the cat's nasal cavity.

Although the cat sort of looks like she's smiling or grimacing when she takes a big whiff, the act of opening the mouth and drawing up the air to the Jacobson's organ is called the flehmen reaction. Essentially, the cat is opening her mouth to suck air into the Jacobson's organ and take a really deep sniff of the odor.

It may look like the cat is offended, but she's probably really enjoying herself. Cats learn all kinds of information about their surroundings through their sense of smell. They mark territory using the scent glands on their cheeks and paws. The glands secrete pheromones, which are chemical substances that stimulate a behavioral response, such as an avoidance or aggressive reaction. Pheromones are also found in saliva, feces, and urine. When cats "spray" it's another way they are marking territory.

The bottom line is that a cat is getting a tremendous amount of information from your living room. All those pieces of furniture she's rubbed up against reveal stories of who has been where when. At our house, to our cats, the floor is undoubtedly a veritable novel of smells revealing stories of humans, canines, and felines wandering all over it.

So when Troi graces us with an open-mouth sniff, she's letting us know that the novel has a particularly exciting moment.

Why Do Cats "Chatter?"

Many people have noticed that when their cat sees a bird through a window, the cat will make a chattering noise. Sometimes they may make small squeaky noises as well. It almost seems like how humans chatter their teeth when they are cold. However, the cat isn't cold. Generally, it happens when the cat sees something he can't get at, so one theory is that the cat is frustrated. The rapid opening and closing of the jaw isn't actually a form of communication.

Another theory is that the action is the same as when a cat kills prey. When a cat attacks, it bites down on the prey several times, which is somewhat like the motion of the chatter. Apparently, the cat is simulating this quick biting action of the kill.

How Smart Are Cats?

As I witness one of my cats staring out the window, I pause to wonder if she is thinking great thoughts. Perhaps she's pondering the meaning of feline existence. (The existential cat!) Maybe she's thinking about dinner. Or maybe she's just staring vacantly off into space and there's a big empty hole where her brain should be. With cats, it's sort of hard to tell.

My cats may not be great thinkers, but I've seen videos of cats that can do all kinds of cool things that definitely require quite a bit of intelligence. Many cats can open doors, drawers, and even some windows. By watching their humans open doors, some cats have figured out that a doorknob needs to be turned clockwise, so they leap up and grab and twist it with their paws. It appears that at least some cats have enough intelligence to observe and imitate actions to get what they want. They also can learn from trial and error.

Although our room doors remain closed, one of our cats has been intrepid enough to figure out how to open some of our kitchen cabinet doors. I can definitely vouch for the trial and error aspect of feline learning behavior. Cats are patient and seem to live by the motto, "if at first you don't succeed, try, try again." Listening to the thump of the kitchen cabinet door all night motivates you to go to the hardware store in the morning and buy baby-proof cabinet locks.

Behaviorists seem to concur that cats do learn and that many aspects of their brains are structurally similar to the human brain. Like humans, cats have short- and long-term memory, so they not only remember when it's time for dinner, they also can recognize people they met years before. Although obviously cats don't read and write, they do learn by example. For example, kittens learn hunting skills by watching their mothers and then practicing the maneuvers themselves. If you've ever seen kittens practicing pouncing on prey, you can tell it requires quite a few tries before they start to get it right.

As anyone who has tried will tell you, training a cat is not like training a dog. Unlike many dogs who live to please their people, cats are monumentally uninterested in what you think.

When it comes to training, the bottom line is that something other than you needs to motivate the cat to do what you want. Otherwise, the cat will just sit and glare at you like you're an idiot. However, some food-motivated cats can be trained using treats.

Clicker training, which involves using food and a click noise as a reward, is often used to train cats to do tricks. So all those cats you see in the movies are probably not particularly different than your cat, except they really like food and have met an incredibly patient trainer.

In the end, cats have many types of problem-solving skills that help them be a cat. If a cat decides that opening a closet door is going to help him get his dinner, he might learn door-opening skills like the cats you see on TV. On the other hand, if he figures it's a lot easier to just wake you up instead, he'll do that. Your cat may be a lot smarter than you give him credit for.

Should I Give My Cat Milk?

Contrary to popular belief, cats shouldn't be fed milk. Obviously kittens get milk from their mother, but after they have been weaned, kittens don't need milk. The milk the kitten gets from her mother is also different from the standard cow's milk you buy in the grocery store. When they are older, cats get all the nutrition they need from food.

Milk is actually generally included on lists of foods you shouldn't feed a cat because it is often hard for cats to digest. Most adult cats do not have sufficient amounts of the enzyme lactase that breaks down the lactose in milk. Like a lot of people, cats are essentially "lactose-intolerant," and this enzyme insufficiency can result in diarrhea. If your cat really enjoys the taste of milk, special lactose free milks especially for pets are available that are easier for cats to digest.

What's a Polydactyl?

Have you ever looked at a cat and thought, "gee, her feet look weird." If so, you were probably looking at a cat equipped with more than the standard number of toes. Most cats have five toes on their front paws and four toes on their rear paws. However, sometimes kittens are born with extra toes. This condition is known as polydactyly.

Sometimes polydactyl cats are referred to as Hemingway cats because the writer Ernest Hemingway wrote about a colony of polydactyls in Florida. Other names include mitten or boxer cats. Some polydactyls have an extra toe that looks like a thumb, and this variety is sometimes known as a thumb cat or cat with thumbs. Some thumb cats can actually use their extra toe as a true opposable thumb to do creative things like pick up stuff.

Polydactyls may have extra toes on just the front paws or on front and rear paws. Some have a different number of toes on each paw. Interestingly, cats never have extra toes on their back paws without having extra toes on their front paws as well. However, cats can have extra toes on their front paws without extra toes on the back.

Apart from their special feet, polydactyl cats are basically just like any other cat. Having extra toes doesn't affect their health or life span. Polydactyly is an inherited trait. In general, the genes that affect polydactyly are dominant, so kittens from a polydactyl mother may have extra toes even if the father does not. Although the offspring from two polydactyl cats are more likely to have extra toes, there's no way to predict how many toes the kittens will have.

If you have a polydactyl, they do require extra foot care. You should pay attention to how the claws grow. The claws on the extra toes have a tendency to curl around and grow into the toe if they aren't trimmed. It depends somewhat on the shape of the toe and where it's located on the paw.

Some people feel that, in general, polydactyls often have a more mellow personality than some other breeds of cat. Although breeding polydactyls can result in more polydactyls, it's not a good idea. In addition to the obvious fact that there are thousands of polydactyl kittens sitting in shelters everywhere, genetics is a tricky thing and trying to breed for more toes can result in deformed cats that can't walk.

If you are thinking of getting a cat, you shouldn't worry about adopting a polydactyl, assuming the cat is healthy in other ways. Kittens with extra toes are adorable with their extra special paws. With a little attention to toe detail, your multi-toed feline can live a long, happy life.

What's with Catnip?

If you've ever seen a cat go nuts for catnip, you may be wondering, "wow, what's in that stuff?" Catnip, or more officially, *Nepetia cataria*, is a plant that's part of the mint family. It's a hardy perennial, which means it's extremely easy to grow, even in North Idaho. I have one catnip plant in my garden that even now is approximately 10 feet tall. I'll be able to make kitty toys for everyone I know if I get organized enough to dry it.

Although scientists haven't exactly figured out what catnip does to cats, they have isolated the substance in catnip that makes your feline friend so happy. The chemical is called nepetalactone and apparently it has an affect on only about 70 percent of cats. Even some big cats like lions are affected. (Now that would be something to see!) Cats also aren't necessarily affected by catnip throughout their lives. Many kittens are immune to it, and some will even avoid catnip.

For cats that are affected by "the nip" it seems like the experience is something pretty great. When you give the susceptible feline a leaf of catnip, first you see the fur ripple as the cat catches that first whiff. Then the cat really gets into it, rolling on the leaves, and zooming around the room. If you have more than one cat, often they'll chase each other and play vigorously. Most of the big action is in the first 5 or 10 minutes. Either exhaustion or burn out sets in and the cat has to nap for a while afterward.

Apparently, the catnip-induced frenzy isn't bad for the cat. Unlike illegal human drugs, which arguably have similar effects, no one has been able to find anything bad about kitty catnip joy. In fact, people have used catnip as a medicinal herb for centuries.

Since we are talking about cats here, yes, it is possible for a cat to get bored with catnip. If you buy every catnip toy in the store, your cat probably won't feel the thrill anymore. But if you use it sparingly, it's cheap entertainment.

One simple toy you can make if you have a bit of catnip is what a friend of mine used to call a "drug rug." You take an old washcloth and sprinkle it with dried catnip. For some reason, it seems like rolling on the drug rug is even more fun for the cat than the normal catnip thrills.

If your cat is susceptible to catnip, you may also discover as we did that catnip is used in some teas. We give our cats boxes to play with after they're empty. We threw an empty box of Celestial Seasonings Tension Tamer tea on the floor for the cats and noticed that one cat stuck her entire head in the box and wandered around.

After that dopey kitty performance, we read the ingredients. And sure enough, there's catnip in there. You can't fool a cat when it comes to catnip.

ALIA

Kitty Spaz Mode

I have often wondered what it is about cats that causes them to suddenly dart around the room erratically. One minute, Fluffy will be completely comatose, snoring on a pillow. The next minute, she's racing around the room seemingly possessed by some demon.

We refer to this kitty behavior as "spaz mode." At some point in time, almost every day, one or more felines in the house enter spaz mode.

Sometimes the onset of spaz mode seems to relate to a lack of food in the food bowl. ("I'm hungry, therefore I spaz.") Other times it seems to relate to a particularly embarrassing kitty failure. ("I fell off the kitty tree; if I spaz maybe no one will notice.") With two cats, we also find spaz mode can relate to a need to dominate the other cat. ("I was reprimanded for jumping on the counter; therefore I will spaz and take out my displeasure on YOU.")

It seems as though cats have no control over spaz mode. Maybe for a cat, spaz mode is like sleep. When a cat needs to sleep, almost nothing gets in her way. Spazzing is the same deal: a cat's gotta do what a cat's gotta do.

What is The "Human–Animal Bond"?

If you love animals, you may have read about the "human–animal" bond. The American Veterinary Medical Association policy defines it as: "a mutually beneficial and dynamic relationship between people and animals that is influenced by behaviors that are essential to the health and well-being of both. This includes, but is not limited to, emotional, psychological, and physical interactions of people, animals, and the environment. The veterinarian's role in the human–animal bond is to maximize the potentials of this relationship between people and animals."

In other words, having pets makes you feel good, both physically and mentally.

Many medical studies have shown that pet owners have lower stress levels and fewer heart attacks. If you have a dog or cat, you always have someone to come home to and your furry friend will never tell your boss all the horrible things you said after a particularly bad day at the office. It should come as no surprise that researchers have found that petting and talking to a companion animal actually reduces blood pressure.

Many people have told me that if they had unlimited space and money, they'd have more pets. I probably would too. But why do people feel so strongly about their pets? Realistically, having pets is a lot of work. I've never seen a scientific explanation why people find pets so appealing. I mean, why is a puppy adorable, even when he's eating your shoe? Why does seeing a cat snoring in a windowsill make you smile?

The bond that forms between a pet and his humans often happens quickly. Even if a person has only had a pet a few weeks, if the pet gets sick, it can be traumatic because the attachment has already formed. The bond increases over time and people often sink into terrible depression after the death of a pet.

You see your pets every day for 10 to15 years. That's a lot more than many people see their relatives, so it's no surprise to feel great loss when your pet is gone. Pet loss support hotlines have become more widely available. In the past, people seemed to think that it wasn't okay to grieve for "just a dog" or "just a cat," but these days you can even buy pet loss sympathy cards.

Many retirement facilities and hospitals bring in pets for visits or have a pet at the facility. It's just more proof that the human–animal bond is special. Every pet is different, but the bond is there.

How Can I Say Goodbye?

For many people, the pets in their household are part of the family. Because of the relatively short life spans of companion animals, at some point, almost all pet owners must make some difficult decisions and then deal with the loss of a pet.

Unfortunately, society often isn't understanding about the feelings of grief people experience when a pet dies. Clichés and sometimes unhelpful advice may make the grieving process more difficult than it has to be. If you viewed your cat as a friend, it's not fair for people to judge your feelings and say, "he was just a cat." The reality is that it's not stupid for you to miss your cat, and you aren't being a "sentimental fool" for grieving for your lost pet. Seven years after she died, I still miss my cat Chani and have a picture of her on my desk.

The decision to euthanize your cat may also complicate the grieving process. When a cat is suffering or unlikely to recover, euthanasia is often decided upon to end a pet's pain. Although this decision is difficult, people need to recognize that sometimes this is the kindest thing we can do for our pets in the final stages of their life. Sometimes understanding more about the process of euthanasia can make the decision less painful. Talk to your veterinarian about what is involved. Some vets will come out to your home, which may be less stressful for you and the cat. Some people may feel they need to be with the cat during the final moments; some do not. When the vet came to euthanize my cat Chani, she actually had been sitting in my lap for many hours beforehand. We gently moved her off my lap to the floor, but I was right next to her.

No matter what you decide, you shouldn't ever feel guilty for all the things you "should have done." After your cat is gone, realize that there will be a gap in your life. Some people think they "hear" their cat wandering around the house or at the door or have dreams about the cat. Grief is a process that can be very difficult to work through. It takes time.

Especially if you have kids, be sure to talk about their feelings. Kids deserve time to accept the loss too, so don't rush out and get another cat. That can give the impression that the pet that died wasn't special. Of course, it's a lot easier to write about this topic than to experience it. There's no way to really completely prepare yourself for the loss of a treasured friend.

Intellectually, we all know that dogs and cats generally only live about 15 years at the most. In fact, I initially wrote this article before my cat Chani died, and it made it no easier when the time came. I was heartbroken and dread the day I have to make that decision again.

It's Worth It

Although you will undoubtedly outlive your pets, that fact shouldn't keep you from enjoying life with a furry friend. I've actually met people that have decided never to own a cat or any other pet because saying goodbye is too "hard." But I think missing out on all those years of companionship is really sad.

I know that I'll always have pets, whether dogs, cats or whatever. I don't want to miss out on the joy of sharing my life and home with a goofy, furry critter. To me, that experience is what it's all about. Although as I mentioned, my cat Chani died at far too young an age, I'm blessed with thousands of memories of the time I shared with her. She spent hours and hours curled up in my lap, and I wouldn't trade that for anything.

If you've read through all the sidebars in this book, you know that adopting my furry feline crew hasn't always been easy. But I know I saved their lives, and in the process, also immeasurably enriched my own.

May your felines make you as happy as Alia, Chani, and Troi have made me.

Index

G

H

I

About the Author

Susan Daffron

Susan Daffron is the President of Logical Expressions, Inc. a publishing company in Sandpoint, Idaho. She also has been a veterinary assistant and worked at animal shelters as an employee and volunteer. She currently owns four dogs and two cats, all of whom came from animal shelters or rescues

Susan has written more than 70 articles that have appeared in national magazines, more than 200 newspaper articles, an online software training course, a software book, cookbook, and book chapters.

In addition to her writing experience, Susan has more than 15 years of experience as a writer, editor, and designer of magazines, newsletters, books and other book-length documents such as users guides and manuals.

She writes articles for her Logical Tips computing site (http://www.logicaltips.com) and for two years published a free (print) computer "how to" magazine, which is archived at http://www.computorcompanion.com. The magazine has evolved into a online quarterly and continues to receive rave reviews from computer users.

Susan also has written more than 200 articles on pet care for her Pet Tails site (http://www.pet-tails.com). She also writes for a site about Sandpoint Idaho (http://www.sandpointinsider. com) and for a newsletter site called Newsletter Help (http://www.newsletterhelp.com).